Acts
of Balance

Profits, People and Place

Grant Copeland

Foreword by **Michael M'Gonigle**

NEW SOCIETY PUBLISHERS

Cataloguing in Publication Data:

A catalog record for this publication is available from the National Library of Canada.

Cover design by Miriam MacPhail from a photograph by Gary Fiegehen.

Printed in Canada on acid-free, partially recycled (20 percent post-consumer) paper using soy-based inks by Transcontinental/Best Book Manufacturers.

New Society Publishers acknowledges the financial support of the Government of Canada through the Book Publishing Industry Development Program (BPIDP) for our publishing activities, and the assistance of the Province of British Columbia through the British Columbia Arts Council.

Paperback ISBN: 0-86571-410-X

Inquiries regarding requests to reprint all or part of *Acts of Balance: Profits, People and Place* should be addressed to New Society Publishers at the address below.

To order directly from the publishers, please add $4.00 shipping to the price of the first copy, and $1.00 for each additional copy (plus GST in Canada). Send check or money order to:

New Society Publishers
P.O. Box 189, Gabriola Island, BC V0R 1X0, Canada

New Society Publishers aims to publish books for fundamental social change through nonviolent action. We focus especially on sustainable living, progressive leadership, and educational and parenting resources. Our full list of books can be browsed on the worldwide web at: http://www.newsociety.com

NEW SOCIETY PUBLISHERS
Gabriola Island BC, Canada

Contents

Acknowledgements

The contents of this book are partly autobiographical because, to a large extent, I based them on my own experience as an environmental and economic planning consultant and entrepreneur. The recommendations in this book are based on pragmatic real-world experience, which would not have been possible without the dedicated efforts of many others. To all of the following individuals I would like to express my sincere thanks.

First of all I would like to acknowledge the privilege of working with many First Nations peoples who, above any others I have encountered in my work, embody the potential for positive changes in the way we conduct our lives and create hope for the collective lives of future generations. In particular, I am grateful for the inspiration I have received from Charles McKay, Collier Azak, Nelson Leeson, Harry Nyce, Rod Robinson, Frank Calder, Joseph Gosnell, Steve Azak, and Hank Moore of the Nisga'a Nation; Gerald Amos, Cecil Paul, James Robertson, John and Beatrice Wilson, Kenny Hall and Charlie Shaw of the Haisla Nation; Alex Bolton and Cliff and Rena Bolton of the Kitsumkalum Band; Ruby Dunstan of the Lytton Band; Miles Richardson and Guu'jau of the Haida Nation; and Bill Webber of the Council for Yukon Indians.

Next, I want to honor my colleagues in the environmental movement, who have inspired me to help protect wilderness and many of whom have showed me how it can be done: David Suzuki, Vicky Husband, Bristol Foster, Michael M'Gonigle and Wendy Wickwire, Ric Careless and Dona Reel, Paul George and Adrienne Carr, Monte Hummel, Jim Fulton, Ray Travers, Sabine Jessen, Colleen McCrory, Wayne McCrory, Elizabeth May, Greg McDade, Dan Culver, Mark Haddock, John Kelson, Thom Henley, Trevor Jones, Trudy Chatwin, Tom Power, Herb and Susie Hammond, Michael Mascall, Tony Pearse, Bill Horswill, Anne Sherrod, Richard Caniell, Peter Rowlands, Josette Wier, Maggie Paquet, and May Murray.

I would also like to recognize my partners in business: my brother Gerry, Roy Trolson, my former wife Helga Copeland, Jim Hagman, Jim Copland, Dennis Holt, Craig Pettitt, John Leontowicz, Peter Leontowicz, Susan and Ian Crichton, Walter and Inga Auschbach, Ellen Kinsel, Ernst and Gretchin Gerwig, and Volker and Cecilia Berlow.

From my years growing up, studying and working in the United States, I would like to acknowledge my early mentors: landscape architect Rich Haag, law professor and my thesis chairman Daniel Mandelker, Ian McHarg, my boss Ron McConnell, and my father Alden Copeland. It was these people who, more than any others, helped get me started.

I would not have written this book without the encouragement and support of my friends Kay Costley-White, who undertook the first edit of the manuscript; Michael M'Gonigle, who peer reviewed and wrote the foreword to this book;

Bristol Foster; Tony Pearse; Bill Horswill; Gary Fiegehen, who contributed many of his photographs, including the cover photo; Trudy Chatwin; Joanne Emily; Jorg and Ulli Becker; Anne Champaigne; Bill Finley and Patrizia Menton; Carolyn Woodward and Jeff George; Lorie Langford and Jeff Bustard, who transferred the text, maps and photographs to computer format; Peter Rowlands and Josette Weir; Maggie Paquet, Barbara Yeomans and Dick Callison; Jon and Lee Ochs, who helped update my computer for this project; and last but far from least, my brother Gerry and his wife Margi, and my son Ryan.

Finally, I would like to extend my sincere appreciation to my hardworking and patient editor, Judith McDowell. Editing of this manuscript was made possible through the financial support of the Eco-Research Chair, University of Victoria, and Vicky Husband of the Sierra Club.

As a personal note, the process of writing this book has been a great benefit to me. One night when I went to bed last November, I was not able to sleep because a pain in my abdomen had intensified. It was similar to the pain I had experienced several years previously, immediately before I had my appendix removed. But the appendix was gone and it had to be something else. This came as a complete surprise. I had been feeling well during the summer and fall months, swimming in the lake and riding my mountain bike or hiking most days.

Two days later, upon awaking from surgery, the doctors informed me that I had colon cancer and that they had removed a large tumor and a section of my large intestine. A few weeks later, after a second surgery and losing over 30 pounds, my prognosis appeared grim. I was told that I would likely live no more than three to six months. If I submitted to six months of chemotherapy, the probability of recovery was 25 percent.

This news caused profound changes in the way I viewed life. My energy levels did not permit me to continue my usual physical activities. So I read a lot and contemplated my life. I became more interested in spiritual matters. I studied the religions of the world, especially Buddhism. Although I very much wanted to continue my life, I also spent considerable time contemplating death and was actively preparing for this possibility.

For many years I had been thinking about writing a book but had never focused on it. Then it occurred to me that I could write it during my chemotherapy. Friends, family, and colleagues encouraged me.

At first, working on the book was difficult; many days I simply did not have any energy to spend on it. On some days I managed to write for an hour or two during the morning. As I slowly regained strength I was gradually able to work more intensively on the project.

Then, after three months of chemotherapy and working on the book, the tumor marker blood tests indicated that the growth of the metastatic tumors which had tethered to the lining of my abdomen and intestines had diminished. I largely attribute this progress to the support from my friends, family, doctors (especially Phil Malpass), and nurses who encouraged me to maintain a positive outlook on life. For their support I am extremely grateful.

Conceiving and implementing community-based economic development projects and processes which are relatively benign environmentally, appropriate socially, and feasible economically, presents a crucially important and difficult challenge that will require a great deal of collaboration and cooperation among many people. To all of you involved in, and committed to, this challenge, I extend my deepest appreciation and encouragement.

New Denver, Summer 1999

"As our century comes to a close and we go toward the beginning of a new millennium, the survival of humanity will depend on our ecological literacy, on our ability to understand these principles of ecology and live accordingly."

Fritjof Capra, *The Web of Life*, 1996

Foreword

To those engaged in the struggle to save Mother Earth, it is becoming increasingly clear that the challenge we face is primarily economic, not environmental. The 1990s were once touted as the world-saving "turnaround decade." Instead, they have been the globalization decade in which a frightening array of exploitative new "free trade" rules and social restrictions have begun to lock up our collective future. A new global constitution is in the making, one that will thrust the grabbing hand of corporate power down into the smallest village and most pristine watershed.

There is, in this struggle, a necessary alternative. Across the planet, a grassroots movement to create the foundations for an ecologically based economy is growing. This movement is composed variously of citizens who respect the land and their community, visionaries who can articulate the shapes of an ecological future, entrepreneurs who can make that future work, and social activists who can help make it happen. At the heart of this movement is the revitalization of community.

Acts of Balance speaks directly to this challenge by drawing on the lessons of experience. In his personal and professional life, Grant Copeland has been all of these things – an imaginative planner of small-scale communities and larger scale cities and valleys; a successful entrepreneur of ecotourism businesses; a wilderness traveller, mapmaker, and advocate; a longtime and engaged resident of the Slocan Valley; and for two decades, a tireless activist with the Valhalla Wilderness Society.

Acts of Balance is, first, a story of Grant's many projects, from his houseboat community in Seattle when he was in graduate school to his pioneering work with the Haisla Nation in carving out a new future for the Kitlope watershed. These projects display an informative diversity. Indeed, I have known Grant for many years now, but reading these tales of his past passions and successes has deepened my respect for a personal life lived wisely and well, and for social contributions made generously and without presumption.

As well as being based on Grant's diverse experiences, this book has a second purpose, as an analysis of how to build an economy rooted in people and place. The problems he identifies – for example, the plethora of inappropriate regulations, or the waste of public resources in a range of "perverse subsidies" – will appeal to a wider audience than the environmental community. Although many in the business community will be interested in these lessons, this is by no means a proposal for free market chaos. Quite the contrary. In making the transition, a huge role exists for a reinvigorated state, but one that is committed first to the sustainability of its peoples/places, and then to rooting profits in that larger objective.

The following pages identify the many "acts of balance" that point to a very different way of seeing the world we inhabit – and making a living in it. The essential message here is that the economic opportunities of the future – a region's "competitive advantage" if you like – exist when local residents steward their resource base, not when nonlocals have the power to plunder it.

This book is, third, an argument, a collective plea, for government officials and politicians, local planners and entrepreneurs, environmentalists and social activists to act in common cause, and to do so now while the natural and social amenities that offer true quality to life still remain for communities to build on. As the recent conflicts and arrests over the protection of domestic watersheds in the Slocan Valley demonstrate, this plea continues to go largely unheard.

Acts of Balance will undoubtedly be controversial. It ventures into difficult terrain: for example, assigning environmental costs to damages that result from business-as-usual, costs (such as those associated with soil erosion caused by clearcut logging) that are very, very difficult to quantify. In addition, this book is a personal reflection, drawing lessons that those who have not faced the author's challenges may not easily understand. For example, the construction of a wilderness lodge that has helped to diversify the local economy also provoked both bureaucratic and environmental conflict. Grant thus confronts not only the difficulties of resisting the old economy, but also the contradictions of actually creating a new one.

To the author's many and diverse achievements, we may now add this book. And if, on reading it, others are moved to help the green economy take deeper root, then *Acts of Balance* could be Grant's most important accomplishment.

Michael M'Gonigle
Eco-Research Professor of Environmental Law and Policy
Faculty of Law and School of Environmental Studies
University of Victoria
Victoria, British Columbia

Acts of Balance
Part 1:

RETHINKING ECONOMY
AND COMMUNITY

Chapter 1

OUR PRESENT DILEMMA AND CHALLENGE

Koyannisqatsi is the Hopi word for "life out of balance" and the name of a film which provides graphic images of the human culture out of touch with the environment. The film contains vivid photography and a mesmerizing sound track by Phillip Glass, but no narration. Unfortunately, the film fails to give us any positive ideas about how we can change to a more environmentally sound and socially appropriate way of living. This is the main purpose of this book – to offer a few examples, based on real-world experience, of how we can begin to make these changes and, in doing so, preserve our cultural and ecological diversity.

Whether we like it or not, we are in a critical period. Most leading ecologists now agree that we will either successfully implement a profound transition in the way we use nature, or we will suffer the consequences of our inaction with the massive extinction – which is already underway – of many life forms on our planet. A sixth biological extinction may be neither a scare tactic nor a radical vision; it is a prospect that we must seriously consider.

We need to look for positive solutions to this issue, examples of people working to preserve biological and cultural diversity and minimize ecological destruction of the natural environment. This book will describe some solutions, but obviously there is a critical need for many more.

Fortunately, we are not faced with total gloom and doom. Citizens all over the world are becoming more aware that we must do a better job of preserving our natural heritage, which includes both cultural and biological diversity. Other positive indicators include the recent increases in small businesses and entrepreneurial activities, and increases in initiatives by individuals. There are a few encouraging signs of economic transitions which are heading in the right direction. This book describes several examples of local community efforts in BC and the US. In general, changes are slower in Canada than south of the border in the United States.

The economic transition which has recently taken place in the states of the Pacific northwest is particularly significant and positive. Sixty-six economists in the Pacific northwest endorsed a report which confirmed that the economic situation in the Pacific northwest is remarkably healthy and vibrant. Changes include significant increases between 1988 and 1994 in the number of jobs (+18%), total personal real income (+24%), total real earnings (+24%), and average real income (+9%) (Pacific Northwest Economists 1995).

Economists, elected officials, and others predicted that logging reductions ordered by the US Supreme Court to save the spotted owl would devastate the

Pacific northwest's economy. They predicted that thousands of workers would be permanently unemployed, their families would be forever destitute, and hundreds of communities would be permanently depressed. The following table and figure show that experience proved otherwise.

Tom Power, Chairman of the Department of Economics at the University of Montana has thoroughly examined one of the reasons for the increase in economic vitality. In his books, *The Economic Pursuit of Quality* and *Lost Landscapes and Failed Economies*, Power argues that because many, if not most, people now have the mobility to choose where they live, work, and retire, preserving quality-of-life is the key to building healthy economies. Many people have been choosing the Pacific northwest states because this area offers relatively desirable places to live. Job availability has become a secondary consideration (Power 1988 and 1996).

Predictions of Massive Unemployment
due to Logging Reductions in the Pacific Northwest Proved to be Wrong:

STUDY	AREA COVERED IN STUDY	PREDICTED DECLINE IN EMPLOYMENT SINCE 1990	ACTUAL CHANGE IN EMPLOYMENT FROM 1990–96
Economic Impact Projections for Alternative Levels of Timber Production in the Douglas-Fir Region (Schallau et al. 1969)	Douglas-fir region (roughly the total Spotted Owl Region)	-211,515	391,682
Final Supplement to the Environmental Impact Statement for an Amendment to the PNW Regional Guide, Volume 1, Spotted Owl Region (USDA 1988)	Oregon and Washington	-175,993	490,499
Economic Impacts of the ISC Northern Spotted Owl Conservation Strategy for Washington, Oregon, and Northern California (Olson 1990)	Spotted Owl Region of Washington, Oregon, and California	-96,645	391,682
Legacy and Promise: Oregon's Forests and wood Products Industry (Beuter 1995)	Oregon	-77,243	229,883
Legacy and Promise: Oregon's Forests and Wood Products Industry, Revised and Updated (Beuter 1998)	Oregon	-42,133	229,883

Source: Niemi, Whitelaw, and Johnston (1999)

Figure 1:
Logging, Employment and Income in Oregon and Washington, 1988-1996

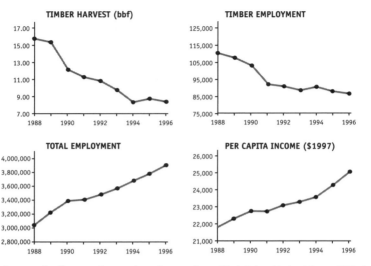

These four graphs illustrate that total employment and per-capita income have increased as timber harvest and employment have decreased.

Source: Niemi, Ernie and Andrew Johnston, ECONorthwest 1999. *The Sky Did Not Fall:* The Pacific Northwest's Response to Logging Reductions, report prepared for Earthlife Canada Foundation and Sierra Club of British Columbia. Secondary sources of information form the Oregon Department of Forestry (various years), the Oregon Employment Department (various years), the US Department of Commerce, Bureau of Economic Analysis (1998), the Washington Department of Natural Resources (various years), and Washington State Employment Security (various years).

The economic transition which is well underway in the US northwest and Canada includes a general maturing of the economy and less dependence on traditional resource-based industries. For example, wood products now represent only 11 percent of the value of the US national forests in Washington and Oregon. The rest, 89 percent, comes from other uses of the forests, including services associated with unroaded areas, camping spots, fishing, and other activities (Haynes and Horne 1997). Under the Northwest Forest Plan, a total of 18.8 million acres have been removed from logging. This has reduced by $4.7 billion the potential sediment-related costs imposed on the general economy (ECONorthwest 1999). The federal government has also realized huge savings in direct subsidies, including the cost of unemployment insurance benefits for workers laid off from Oregon's lumber and wood products industry. These benefits exceeded by more than $249 million the premiums paid by the industry (Clark 1994). Between 1983 and 1994, the timber-sale programs of 20 national forests in eastern Oregon, eastern Washington, and Idaho consistently failed to yield a positive return to the national treasury. For the period as a whole, total government expenditures exceeded returns to the Treasury by $1.3 billion (Wolf 1994).

A study by US Forest Service economists documented that society values recreational resources three to four times more than the sum of timber, grazing, and mining resources (Haynes 1992). A nationwide survey indicated that respondents believed that the benefits of protecting the old-growth, spotted-owl forests would be between 3.5 and 14.1 times greater than the costs (Hagen, Vincent, and Welle, 1992). A study by the Oregon-based economic consulting firm ECONorthwest provides compelling evidence that the traditional economic base model no longer accurately reflects reality and that the grossly inflated multipliers assigned to traditional resource industries are no longer valid (Niemi and Johnson 1999).

There is a growing consensus among serious students of the present global ecological situation that we simply cannot continue on our present course of population and economic growth and that we need an alternate paradigm. In 1983, the United Nations set up the World Commission on Environment and Development, headed by Gro Harlem Brundtland. The Commission re-examined the critical environmental and development problems on planet Earth and formulated realistic proposals for change. In 1987, after four years of exhaustive study by the world's leading scientists, activists and political leaders, the Commission published a comprehensive report entitled *Our Common Future*. The report served notice that the time had come for a marriage of economy and ecology. Unfortunately, twelve years later, we remain locked onto our path of unsustainable growth and increasing globalization of the world economy.

Balance is about sustainability, but it is also about sharing resources. Although the United Nations again ranked Canada the best country in the world for the sixth straight year, we have much room for improvement, especially in the sharing of wealth. (Globe and Mail July 12, 1999) The UN Human Development Index balances income performance with a country's achievements in health and education. The 1999 UN report focuses on the increasing worldwide gap between rich and poor caused by the forces of economic globalization. "Global inequalities in income and living standards have reached grotesque proportions." The assets of the 200 richest people on Earth, which grew to $1,042 billion in 1998 from $440 billion in 1994, are more than the combined income of 41 percent of the world's population, according to the UN report. Most significantly, these 200 people more than doubled their net worth to $1 trillion in only four years (1994 to 1998).

One-fifth of the world's people live in countries with the highest incomes. They now produce 86 percent of the world's gross domestic product and 82 percent of foreign direct investment. The income gap between the richest fifth of the world's countries and the poorest fifth, measured by average national income per person, increased from 30 to 1 in 1960 to 74 to 1 in 1997. According to David Korten, who holds a Ph.D. from Stanford University's Business School and who served on the faculty of Harvard University's Business School, if we take into account the very rich people who live in poor countries and the very poor people who live in rich countries, the incomes of the richest 20 percent of the world's people are approximately 150 times higher than those of the poorest 20 percent (Korten 1966).

Robert Reich is a leading political economist in the US. He is a member of the faculty of Harvard's Kennedy School of Government and serves as Secretary of Labor for the Clinton administration. In his book *The Work of Nations*, Reich describes what he calls "symbolic analysts," people who are effective in solving, identifying, or brokering problems. These highly skilled persons are capturing more and more of the total global income and are in high demand internationally, while those who are less skilled and less educated are receiving less and less of the total global income because of a decline in the need for unskilled labor. (Reich 1992) A recent example of this trend is internet commerce, which is currently doubling approximately every nine months. Many "symbolic analysts" are effective users of information for the purpose of making money.

The rapid globalization of the world economy benefits transnational corporations at the expense of community-based economies, especially in developing countries. No more than five corporations now control more than 50 percent of the global markets for consumer durables, automotive products, airlines, aerospace, electronic components, electricity and electronics, and steel. No more than five firms control over 40 percent of the global markets for oil, personal computers, and media (Korten 1996). From a global perspective, a monopoly usually means a situation in which fewer than four or five corporations control more than 40 percent of the market for a particular commodity (e.g., E. Goldsmith 1996). By this definition, a very large part of global production is now monopolistic, making it increasingly difficult for smaller firms to compete.

These largest firms are shedding the most jobs. The Fortune 500 firms reduced employment by 4.4 million between 1980 and 1993. During this period, their sales increased 1.4 times, assets increased 2.3 times, and compensation for CEOs increased 6.1 times (Korten, 1996). The average compensation for CEOs in the US has increased from 12 times the wage of the average factory worker in 1960 to about seventy times a factory worker's wage at the end of the 1980s (Reich 1992).

Transnational corporations account for 47 of the top 100 economies in the world. The remainder are still nation-states. Transnational companies are increasingly dominating the global economy. Five hundred corporations control 70 percent of global trade, and a mere one percent of transnational corporations own half of foreign direct investment. These alarming statistics illustrate a massive shift in power from national governments to transnational corporations (Reich 1992; Clarke 1996).

As a result of the General Agreement on Tariffs and Trade (GATT), third-world countries are now under an obligation to accept all investments from abroad. Private investment in the third world currently runs about $200 billion a year. This amount dwarfs the World Bank's until-now contribution of about $23 billion per year (E. Goldsmith 1996).

An example of the globalization of the economy is the bid by Weyerhauser, already one of the largest logging companies in the world and the largest private landholder in the United States, to take over MacMillan Bloedel, the largest producer of forest products in Canada and one of the largest landowners in BC. In addition to further concentrating control of the international forest industry, this proposed takeover brings into question the compensation requirements under the North American Free Trade Agreement (NAFTA) that affect the ability of Canadian federal and provincial governments to make major land-use decisions, such as First Nations treaty settlements and forest tenure reform. It could create difficulties in negotiating aboriginal treaties and reducing logging to ecologically sustainable levels by requiring Canadian governments to compensate American corporations for lost earnings.

The large transnational corporations control most of the world's advertising. One hundred corporations pay for 75 percent of commercial broadcast time and thereby dominate the commercial channels. In addition, they finance 50 percent of public television. The average US viewer watches 22,000 commercials every year (Mander 1996).

For every dollar circulating in the productive economy today, $20 to $50 circulates in the world of finance. Since these transactions take place through unmonitored international computer networks linked by fiber optics and satellite transmissions, no one knows how much is really involved. The $1 trillion that changes hands each day in the world's international currency markets is 20 to 30 times the amount required to cover daily trade in actual goods and services (Korten 1996). Most worrisome, the collapse of the Mexican economy in 1994-95 and the recent Asian economic crisis (1998-99) are signs that global finance has been growing increasingly out of control. Neither the most powerful and richest countries or the largest banks can control the instantaneous flow of capital around the world and effectively counter the worse economic crises that are bound to come.

The chief executive officers and chief financial officers of the largest corporations and global financial traders are relentlessly pushing the world past the sustainable limits of its finite resources. For them the bottom line is increasing their corporate profits and returns on investment. Because of this, former World Bank economist Herman Daly has called sustainability in a growth-dependent globalized economy an impossibility theorem.

So what is the alternative? According to Daly, Korten, and others who have examined this question, the answer lies in the opposite direction of globalization, towards much smaller and more ecologically sustainable alternative economies.

The key question this book addresses is: how do we reverse the trend toward globalization? Here in Canada, local, regional, provincial, and national governments have not provided definitive economic development guidelines for entrepreneurs and communities. Instead of benefiting the small, community-based businesses that have been creating the majority of new jobs, most government subsidies and bank loans have gone to the larger corporations that have been shedding the most jobs.

Many, if not most, environmental groups have avoided supporting economic development, regardless of the size of the project. These well-meaning organizations have tended to resist most development proposals.

Despite large recent declines in the membership of labor unions, most labor organizations have concentrated their collective efforts on protecting the status quo and the high paying jobs of their remaining members. Forest industry workers in BC receive relatively high wages. However, these workers often experience difficulties switching to jobs outside the forest industry. One survey (Goetz, et al 1991) revealed that 55.9 percent of workers in eight sawmills across British Columbia either could not deal with material written at the grade 4 to 5 level or needed help with it. Since many of these workers are now in their 40s and 50s, they are finding it difficult to earn as much elsewhere. A study commissioned by the Western Wood Products Forum found that of forest industry workers laid off between 1979 and 1985, most did not regain employment within the forest industry and, as a consequence, suffered a drop in income of 27-33 percent (Cohen and Allen 1988).

Herein lies a significant difference between BC and the Pacific northwest states. In the Pacific northwest states, average forest industry wages have dropped from $38,000 in 1991 to $32,000 (US dollars) per year as the demand for workers, especially those with relatively low skill levels, has diminished with the reduction in logging. In BC, the powerful IWA has managed to resist wage decreases. The union also maintains a huge influence on the provincial government regarding the logging of forests in BC. As a result, government attempts to make significant reductions in the annual cut, improve forest practices, or increase the value added to forest products have been extremely slow in coming.

In terms of real commitments, the forest industry, the IWA, and governments have usually resisted attempts to formulate effective economic transition strategies based on ecologically sustainable parameters. Environmental groups have primarily occupied themselves with ecological concerns and have avoided addressing economic issues. None of these interests has offered a vision that would integrate the need for new economic development with the need to preserve ecological integrity.

Most economic development projects cannot meet all environmental, social, and economic criteria perfectly. This book describes a few examples, of "acts of balance" that hold the promise of reconciling these three criteria. The challenge facing us today is to define what is an acceptable balance of community-based and global economic development, and then find ways to support this new "green economy." Unless we make significant positive changes in the way we treat economic development, we will continue to drift further and further out of balance.

Chapter 2

The Economy of Place: It Works

The International Society for Ecological Economics defines the relatively new field of ecological economics as the "combined study of human ecology and the economy of nature, the web of interconnections uniting the economic subsystem to the global ecosystem of which it is a part" (Costanza 1991). Ecological economics has largely evolved since the publication in 1987 of *Our Common Future*, the report of the World Commission on Environment and Development. The commission's central recommendation was a transition to "sustainable development," defined as "meeting the needs of the present without compromising the ability of future generations to meet their own needs." The commission argued that people have the capacity to build a future that is "more prosperous, more just, and more secure." Although the report documented "ever increasing environmental decay, poverty, and hardship in an ever more polluted world with diminishing resources," the commission saw a possibility for a "new era of economic growth, one that must be based on policies that sustain and expand the environmental resource base." The commission also regarded this kind of growth as "absolutely essential to relieve the great poverty that is deepening in much of the developing world."

The commission based its hope for the future on "decisive political action now to begin managing environmental resources to ensure both sustainable human progress and human survival." It is now 12 years since the commission published its report, and we have seen very little political commitment or significant progress towards achieving ecological sustainability.

Today, economic growth is running rampant without regard for ecological limits or the distribution of wealth, which flows increasingly to the richest people. Most nations have reneged on the environmental commitments their leaders made during the Rio summit on the environment in 1992. Everywhere in the world, people continue to use more and more energy, and most nations, including Canada, have failed to implement legislation to protect endangered species. Although Canada has adopted the World Commission on Environment and Development's suggestion to protect 12 percent of the land base, most provinces have been extremely slow to implement this modest goal, according to reports by the World Wildlife Fund (Hummel 1989 and subsequent reports).

In the introduction to the book *Ecological Economics*, Robert Costanza, Herman Daly, and Joy Bartholomew describe an ecological economic world view which includes "an increasing awareness that our global ecological life support system is endangered and forcing us to realize that decisions made on the basis of local, narrow, short-term criteria can produce disastrous results globally and in the long run" (Costanza 1991). Their presumption that local decisions usually lead to disastrous results is misleading at a time when we need more local control and more community-based economic development. Part 2 of this book argues for more emphasis on and support for community-based economic development and a reduction in the globalized economy.

Costanza's book does not provide many real-world examples of how we can make the transition to an economy based on ecological limits, or examples of compromises between economic, ecological, and social factors. It does, however, make a convincing case for merging the disciplines of economics and ecology into a new transdisciplinary field of study that addresses the relationships between ecosystems and economic systems.

What we need is a reasonable level of flexibility in order to be able to implement better or good projects without compromising the ecological bottom line. By advocating flexibility and compromise, I am not advocating compromising ecological integrity or decreasing biological or cultural diversity. To me, these qualities constitute the ecological bottom line.

The International Society for Ecological Economics offers a definition of ecological economics that encompasses both biological and cultural change. Robert Costanza, Herman Daly, and Joy Bartholomew make the important point that biological evolution is slow relative to cultural evolution (Costanza 1991). Biological evolution thus contains a built-in, long-run constraint that cultural evolution does not have. Before they were exposed to western thinking, most traditional aboriginal cultures were much more in tune with the limits of their natural environment. We can learn a great deal about sharing, respecting elders, supporting young people, and respecting the land from aboriginal people who remain in touch with their traditional cultures. In Part 4, we will examine two examples of how First Nations are working to provide balanced and appropriate economic opportunities for their people. Because they have not lost the values inherent in their traditional culture, some of their economic development projects are both socially appropriate and relatively benign environmentally.

Costanza, Daly, and Bartholomew argue that "if humans are to manage the whole planet effectively, we must develop the capacity to take a broader biocentric perspective and to treat our fellow species with respect and fairness" (Costanza 1991). They make an important distinction between "growth" and "development." As they put it, "economic growth, which is an increase in quantity, cannot be sustainable indefinitely on a finite planet. Economic development, which is an improvement in the quality-of-life without necessarily causing an increase in quantity of resources consumed, may be sustainable. Sustainable growth is an impossibility."

Costanza, Daly and Bartholomew define sustainability as "the amount of consumption that can be continued indefinitely without degrading capital stocks – including 'natural capital' stocks. In a business, capital stock includes long-term assets such as buildings and machinery. Natural capital is the soil, atmospheric structure, plant and animal biomass, etc., that, taken together, form the basis of all ecosystems." They point out that we have entered a new era in which the limiting factor in development is no longer man-made capital but remaining natural capital. "Timber is thus limited by remaining forests, not sawmill capacity . . ." "Sustainability is a relationship between dynamic human economic systems and larger dynamic, but normally slower-changing ecological systems, in which 1) human life can continue indefinitely, 2) human individuals can flourish, and 3) human cultures can develop; but in which effects of human activities remain within bounds, so as not to destroy the diversity, complexity, and function of the ecological life support system" (Costanza, 1991).

Costanza, Daly, and Bartholomew's definition of sustainability is significantly closer to the concept of ecologically sustainable development than the definition offered by the World Commission on Environment and Development: that is, "economic growth . . . based on policies that sustain and expand the environmental resource base." We need to do more to help the citizens and entrepreneurs of the world decide what is ecologically sustainable. The central thesis of this book is that we, the public, must decide what constitutes an acceptable balance between these two divergent concepts. We will need to find compromises while we make the transition from the World Commission's political view to the more ideal ecological view. We will also need to make a much greater commitment towards the rapid development of a more evolved political ecology.

According to Michael M'Gonigle of the University of Victoria, this political ecology will probably include an:

> "overall character of economic development away from free-trade-based regimes towards community-based forms of territorial self-maintenance. These forms include a wide range of cutting-edge technical-scientific innovations – eco-forestry, ecosystem-based planning and management, demand management, precautionary principle, clean technology, industrial ecology – which embody a different set of starting principles than the 'laws' of the competitive market, and a very different set of process and power elements to them. Huge transformations are in store as the industrial model that is today based on creating ever more supply – in energy, water, transportation, even agriculture – is shifted to managing the linear nature of demand" (M'Gonigle, 1999).

M'Gonigle argues that the primary lesson of ecological economic science is the need to create new political contexts that will shift economic activity from linear to circular processes of wealth-generation, at which point economic "values" will begin to have a more relevant and inclusive meaning. Secondly, we need to explicitly address and effectively integrate the political/power context for economic activities. If we are unsuccessful in making these changes, the current out-of-control globalized economy will continue its quest for economic domination, and environmental and social values will continue to be subordinated to the maximization of corporate profits.

Fritjof Capra puts it another way. He suggests that we all must become more ecologically literate:

"To be ecologically literate, we must understand the basic principles of ecology. This means understanding the principles of organization of ecological communities (ecosystems) and use those principles for creating sustainable human communities. We need to revitalize our communities – including our educational communities, business communities, and political communities – so that the principles of ecology become manifest in them as principles of education, management, and politics. This requires shifts of perception that are characteristic of systems thinking – from the parts to the whole, from objects to relationships, from contents to patterns. A sustainable human community is aware of the multiple relationships among its members. Nourishing the community means nourishing those relationships" (Capra 1996).

Capra points out that cyclical processes are an important principle of ecology. A major conflict between economics and ecology stems from the fact that nature is cyclical, whereas our industrial systems are linear. To induce our industrial systems to follow cyclical patterns, we will need to redesign the way we conduct business. As Capra explains it, "Economics emphasizes competition, expansion, and domination; ecology emphasizes cooperation, conservation, and partnership."

Acts of Balance
Part 2:

COMMUNITY-BASED ECONOMIC DEVELOPMENT

Overview

Promoting and supporting community-based development is an important method for shifting to an ecologically sound economy. The residents of a community usually initiate, finance, implement, and control community-based economic development. Because most local residents care about the quality of life in their communities, long-term ecological sustainability, and long-term employment for their families, they are likely to be better stewards of their environment than remote governments seeking maximum tax revenues or large corporations seeking maximum return on investment and continuous growth in profits.

A community with a diversified local economy composed of many small-scale enterprises will enjoy more social and economic stability than a single-industry community that is vulnerable to boom-and-bust cycles and rapidly changing technologies. Community-based economic development is a preferable alternative to increasing economic globalization, primarily because people have more control over community-based business enterprises than they have over large multinational corporations. For these reasons, local communities that are willing to assume this level of responsibility should take control of local resources.

Unless local communities take more control over their environments, social services, and economies, they will face increasing outside control, indiscriminate exploitation of local resources, and loss of jobs. Local control means that the people who live in a community decide what mix of economic activities will best serve environmental, social, and economic values. Local control presents a formidable challenge to communities, but control by provincial and national governments and large corporations will make it harder to develop economic strategies that achieve an optimum mix of these three factors. Community-based economic development requires cooperation and collective effort from local residents. Because a project is rarely perfect in all three ways – environmentally, socially, and economically – economic development usually requires establishing a balance among environmental management, job creation, and economic returns to entrepreneurs and/or shareholders of companies.

13

"In every community there will invariably be contradictions and conflicts, which cannot be resolved in favour of one or the other side. For example, the community will need stability and change, order and freedom, tradition and innovation. Rather than by rigid decisions, these unavoidable conflicts are much better resolved by establishing a dynamic balance. Ecological literacy includes the knowledge that both sides of a conflict can be important, depending on the context, and that the contradictions within a community are signs of its diversity and vitality and thus contribute to the system's viability. In ecosystems, the complexity of the network is a consequence of its biodiversity, and thus a diverse ecological community is a resilient community. In human communities ethnic and cultural diversity may play the same role. Diversity means many different relationships, many different approaches to the same problem. A diverse community is a resilient community, capable of adapting to changing situations" (Capra 1996).

Although there are advantages inherent in community-based planning and management of public resources, development proposals usually generate conflict, no matter how well they are designed or the extent to which they represent a balance between social, economic, and ecological considerations. In some cases, objections are based on selfish concerns, but they can also stem from genuine commitment to social or environmental issues that affect entire communities. Objections can also be based on erroneous information and analysis. Resolving these conflicts involves negotiation and compromise.

Active democracy at the village, town, and rural area level offers the best avenue for resolving disagreements on development issues. In a general sense, the smaller the political body, the more accountable and responsible to its constituents it is likely to be and the more likely people will listen to and consider each other's concerns. The more closely people are directly involved with the land and the place they live, the better collective stewards they can be of the community's interest. (There are notable exceptions to this, such as President Roosevelt's initially unpopular and secret decision to enter World War II in the alliance against Hitler, or the Canadian parliament's denial of further commercial development in Banff National Park despite protest from local government representatives.) Democratic decision making is much less successful at the national and international level because special interest groups, equipped with the time and money to lobby elected representatives, tend to distort political outcomes and public policy. In fact, involvement with state or provincial governments on development issues can be problematic because communities usually do not have the kind of political influence that can command the attention of elected representatives. Community-based economic development often involves struggling to make senior governments at the provincial or state level respond to local preferences.

Involvement in community-based economic development "instills a sense of connection with the place we live" and "ultimately a spiritual awakening that comes from making a connection to others and to nature" (Norberg-Hodge 1996). First Nations have long recognized a close connection with place. As Jeannette Armstrong from the Penticton Band in BC eloquently describes it, "Community is formed by people who are acting in cooperation with each other. Each person is cared for because each is bound to someone else through emotional ties, and all in the community are bound by generations of interactions with one another" (Armstrong 1996). Part 4 outlines two examples of First Nations leadership taking control of resource management and economic development.

There are exceptions to the preference for smaller, community-based economic development, particularly in situations that require financing and development efforts which exceed the capacities of local communities. Economic development projects that originate outside the community can be acceptable if they encompass broad environmental, social, and economic criteria that meet local needs. But generally, economic development should not default to the global level if it can succeed at the community level. (Chapter 13 describes two acceptable larger green projects.)

While most communities today will not be able to produce everything they need, communities can develop self reliance by replacing many imported products with locally produced products. Import substitution is particularly important in agriculture where it includes buying food from local farmers who may have to charge more because they are producing in short, northern growing seasons or in expensive greenhouses instead of buying produce from growers working in more favorable climates in California and Mexico. Opportunities for import substitution are usually obvious and plentiful – small local hydro projects; locally produced building materials, homes and furniture; maintaining automobiles locally to extend their use, and many other possibilities.

Import substitution is just one aspect of community-based economic development. We usually use the term to refer to a project or process at the community level that local residents are directing and controlling.

Government and nongovernment organizations initiate some community-based projects such as constructing public hiking and biking trails, developing public infrastructure such as roads and bridges, conducting planning processes, or providing services such as health care and training. However, these projects and programs are not the main concern of community-based economic development. Public projects are needed and beneficial, but financing usually comes from tax revenues, and control ultimately remains in the hands of a government agency. Private enterprises are usually more challenging to finance and operate. Private enterprises generate tax revenue and are the source of funding for most public enterprises. For these reasons, this book focuses primarily on private enterprise examples.

Part 2 contains three different examples of community-based economic development. The first case study describes the experience of implementing a small houseboat development project in Seattle, a project designed to increase neighborhood identity and community involvement in design. The other two projects are currently in the process of implementation and are located in the Slocan Valley, a rural area in southeastern BC. The second case study describes the 25-year-long community effort to transform and downsize local logging practices to a more sustainable, ecosystem-based level. The third case study is an eight-year attempt by a local mining family to diversify into tourism by developing a small-scale, all-season resort. Detailed examination of these three projects reveals astonishing governmental controls and resistance to small-scale business development and local control of resources. These three processes are not atypical – they are representative of what is happening in many communities in North America.

Chapter 3

PORTAGE-AT-BAY:
A COMMUNITY THAT FLOATS

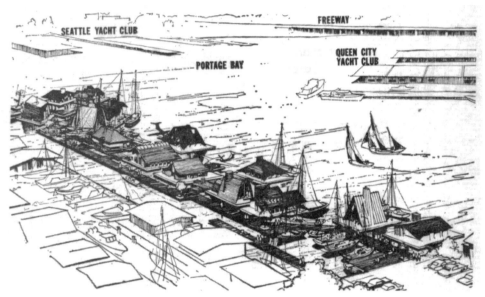

Artist's rendering of Portage-at-Bay, an experiment in increasing oportunities for neighbourhood-scale community involvement.

In 1967, I lived in Seattle, a beautiful city which fronts on Puget Sound, surrounds Lake Union and Portage Bay, and borders Lake Washington. While living there, I was drawn to the water and to the idea of living on a houseboat. For a century or more, a small number of Seattle's residents had chosen this life style. One of my artist friends lived on a houseboat in Seattle in a manner that was Bohemian, refreshing, full of life, and close to the nautical nature of the city. When I visited him, I sensed that he identified to an unusual degree with the place he lived, and that his home accommodated a fierce feeling of independence and freedom, a quality he shared with most of his neighbors.

I moved out of my apartment and bought an older houseboat that floated on cedar logs. It was tied up along the south bank of the ship canal which links the inland lakes with the sea. Even though my moorage was insecure and I could have been evicted on very short notice, I loved the dynamic feeling of living on the water. I enjoyed the smells and the sounds of the waterfront, with its flocks of shorebirds and many pairs of ever-present Canadian geese. Especially alluring were the sounds of boats passing close by, the rocking motion from their wakes, and the colorful and changing reflections off the water. One of Seattle's larger tug boat companies had a base next to our moorage, and our dock also accommodated an interesting mix of ancient fishing boats, barges, and sailboats, as well as houseboats. It had character. As a graduate student in urban planning, I wondered if it would be possible to emulate these qualities of houseboat living in a more secure moorage and to design such a development using a combination of marine architecture, local Pacific northwest design motifs, and a nautical scale.

Portage-at-Bay was my first experience as a young entrepreneur. The idea of developing a new houseboat dock in Seattle was not only the natural outcome of living in an old turn-of-the-century houseboat; it was also a response to the City of Seattle's unwritten policy of banishing its historic and colorful houseboat colonies from the urban landscape. The city's policy did not make sense to me because the houseboats offered a unique way of life and were also one of Seattle's most popular tourist attractions.

I spent many days and evenings exploring the waterfront in a small dinghy and eventually located a 1.2 acre underwater lot that was already zoned for houseboat use. The site is located across from the Seattle and Queen City yacht clubs in Portage Bay, south of the University of Washington. My motivation was to help revitalize the aging houseboat moorages by building a new dock and new houseboats. The idea was also influenced by the need to build a sense of identity among houseboat dwellers by creating a common dock that would tie residents together and encourage them to meet and communicate with one another on a daily basis.

Theoretically, in a free and open society, nothing would inhibit people from designing and producing the kind of housing they want. Anyone who desired to live in a prefabricated plastic spaceship cabin, or a half-timber Gothic house, could do so. In practice, however, societies are neither free nor unregulated. In urban areas, planning officials are likely to interpret unconventional, nonstandard dwellings as nonconforming or incompatible with surrounding buildings. The problem of over-regulation becomes even more challenging in relation to a larger-scale development that incorporates multiple dwellings.

Originally, codes and ordinances were supposed to protect people from physically unsafe structures, but these controls have often placed little importance on intangible quality of life issues such as a sense of identification and belonging, community involvement, or people's unique personal needs.

Portage-at-Bay illustrated how negative controls and institutional constraints can inhibit innovations in environmental design and community development. By examining the process of implementing this project, we can gain some understanding of why developers are so often reluctant to experiment with ways of improving their projects.

The objective of the Portage-at-Bay project was to provide a new and different type of housing. The concept involved designing dwellings to provide a maximum

Houseboats at Portage-at-Bay, a great place to live in the centre of a city.

relationship with the water – a natural style of housing for Seattle.

My brother Gerry and I and a third partner were the developers. In an effort to generate maximum individual identity, we gave the architects a lot of design freedom. Because Seattle had no building codes for houseboats, the designers, who included my brother, were able to work with relatively few limitations. However, as the developers, we tried to ensure that the overall design of the project was consistent in quality, materials, and nautical scale.

Separating pedestrians from vehicles as much as possible was an important element of the design philosophy. We accomplished this by locating the parking lot on land rather than on a wharf over the water. However, this decision created problems for us because although it was legal to park on a wharf, an onshore parking lot violated several of the legal absolutes in the zoning ordinance.

Although the zoning for the property permitted houseboats, the building permit required a conditional use permit for the accessory parking lot because it was located across an unimproved street from the underwater property where the houseboats were to be moored. The zoning regulations also required several side yard and screening variances.

The notice for a public hearing before the Board of Adjustment upset some of the neighbors, who opposed development of the privately owned vacant underwater lot. They believed that the project would bring down the value of their property. At the hearing, the Board of Adjustment cut the proposed development from 14 houseboats to eight (22 would have been legal with an over-the-water parking lot). But the neighbors, still not satisfied, appealed the matter to the City Council.

Later they dropped the appeal on the day of the scheduled council hearing and initiated legal action against the City Building Department. The neighbors lost the court case, but they had managed to stall the development of the project for nearly six months. We would have had a tough time surviving the legal process if my brother and I had not had a third partner who was an attorney.

The opposition from the neighbors could be interpreted as "community-based," and in fact it would appear to contradict my arguments in favor of community-based economic development projects. However, I believe that the opposition was, for the most part, based on erroneous information from a few neighbors who saw the project as a threat to the value of their property. In addition, there could have been no opposition to the project if we had elected to build the parking lot on a wharf over the water because this would have satisfied the legal requirements of Seattle's zoning bylaw. Instead we wanted to build according to what we believed was a better solution. Finally, the neighbors would probably not have filed the writ of mandamus if they had had to pay the legal costs. Because the opponents of the project had filed the writ of mandamus against the City of Seattle for its intention to issue a building permit, the plaintiffs were not liable for any of the costs of litigation or for any costs associated with delaying the project. As a result, the neighbors had very little to lose by stalling our project in court.

Stalled by the delay in securing the site improvement permit, we were running short of development capital, and we still had the problem of financing the construction of the prototype houseboat. Because the project did not follow the norm of conventional construction and because we had no previous experience as builders, it was not easy to get financing. We spent nearly a month attempting to secure a loan from larger banks and saving and loan associations before we found a community bank which took the trouble to evaluate our proposal carefully before deciding to grant our loan.

But this was not the end of our problems. Although the city's Building Department told us at the beginning of the project that houseboat construction did not require building permits, when we were nearly finished building the prototype, the city building inspectors told us that we would have to conform to the city's electrical and plumbing codes.

Another issue involved sewage disposal. At the time the City of Seattle discharged sewage and storm drainage from approximately ten overflows into Lake Union and Portage Bay during heavy runoff periods. However, the city made us agree to collect our sewage with an underwater gravity line and pump it into the city sewers. Because we were dealing with an unusual situation and because we wanted to create the best possible product, we intended to use plastic plumbing pipe: it was both less expensive and the best material available for residential plumbing – particularly in a marine application. Although this kind of pipe was illegal for use in the City of Seattle at the time, we used it anyway, and it has worked fine.

Because we wanted to put all the utilities out of sight under the dock, we need-

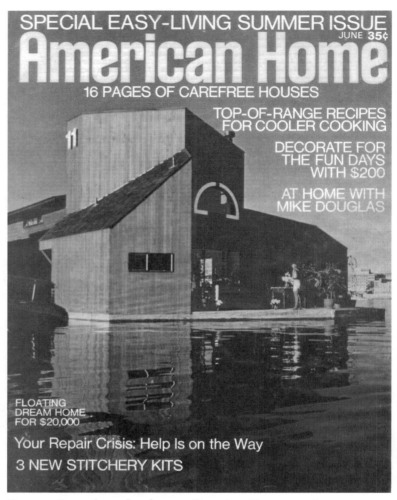

Portage-at-Bay, as featured on the cover of American Home *magazine*

ed a flexible electrical connection under the gangplanks, but the city's electrical code did not allow this, even though the city itself had installed a similar under-the-dock electrical system at its large Sho-Sho Marina. We fought several battles on issues such as these, some of them involving interjurisdictional disputes between different public agencies. We managed to resolve most of the hassles, but never without expending a great deal of effort, money, and time.

There is no single solution to the challenge of creating innovations in environmental design and implementing more practical methods of construction. Thirty years ago, after the successful implementation of the project, I advocated a number of alternatives in an article published in the Seattle Times. My suggestions included more flexible mortgages for innovative projects. Without this kind of flexibility from private sources of financing, developers of innovative projects would probably need to look for government funding.

I also argued for more flexible building codes to accommodate new types of building materials and more efficient construction techniques. Replacing rigid zoning ordinances with flexible performance standards would allow a wider variety of solutions to the problems that zoning regulations seek to control. For example, in some jurisdictions, comprehensive plans and zoning bylaws contain regulatory provisions that would permit site planning alternatives such as cluster housing, which minimizes the need for roads and services and retains more park land in development sites.

These recommendations are still relevant today.

Houseboats are not a panacea for the needs of all those who prefer not to live in a suburban rambler or an anonymous city apartment. For example, couples who have raised their children and who desire an active life in the city without the chores of yard maintenance and daily commuting also need environmental innovations. Younger people who tend to share residential units need creative solutions. We need new techniques for housing the elderly and married students. Many people want a closer relationship to their environment than an apartment or a condominium can provide. But we need experiments and innovations; mere theoretical ideas are not enough.

Building codes need to change from a method of regulating construction into a new system for improving environments for living. If we expect to develop a better product, we must remove institutional constraints and replace them with sound planning principles backed by performance standards designed to meet the various objectives of the ultimate consumer, the public.

If we supplied them with a language of sound performance standards and planning principles, professional planners, architects, and engineers could take on more administrative authority and responsibility. Although these professionals can also be conventional in their design work, at least the more innovative and creative ones would have the option of proposing alternatives. This delegation of design responsibilities would be more effective than the common practice, which requires that legislative bodies approve nearly all critical planning and land-use decisions and that building inspectors who lack training in architecture and engineering make decisions about how buildings should be constructed. In addition to a concern about public safety, we need a commitment to esthetics and an environment that can help people create a sense of community. If we replaced the existing law, which consists of rigid, absolute rules with sound performance standards and planning principles, the courts would have something more meaningful to turn to in deciding development issues.

In the end, Portage-at-Bay was successful on a number of counts. First of all, many national publications recognized the project and featured it prominently. These included Fortune magazine in a special issue on the environment, the

Seattle Times, and American Home magazine, which gave it a cover story, as well as other publications.

In addition, a group of builders from Japan flew to Seattle to view the project, and the Fiberboard Corporation, a large real estate development company based in California, investigated the concept. Executives from the company came to Seattle to see the project and afterwards, the company flew me down to their corporate headquarters for further consultation. Although they would have liked to emulate Portage-at-Bay on waterfront property the company owned in San Francisco Bay, they saw too many obstacles and decided that successful implementation would involve too much risk.

The success of the project proved that the resistance in the neighborhood was mistaken in predicting a depreciation in property values. In fact, the value of most of the new houseboats exceeded the values of neighborhood homes and actually caused appreciation of the upland properties. Most important, the project proved to be successful in terms of giving residents an unusual degree of community identity. An ex-post-facto survey by the University of Washington Architecture and Planning School questioned residents living at Portage-at-Bay and other city environments. The results indicated that people living at Portage-at-Bay identify more strongly with their environment than people in other neighborhoods and that they were significantly more involved in the creation of their environment (Copeland 1969).

The Portage-at-Bay experiment points to some of the changes which are needed in order to stimulate more innovation in land-use development. In this connection, the overriding concerns have to do with the need for flexibility and careful, unbiased consideration of the merits of progressive development proposals. Positive approaches that encourage and support optimum solutions are preferable to negative ones that favor convention and mediocrity.

Chapter 4

SLOCAN VALLEY:
THE PEOPLE'S FOREST

Grant Copeland

*Slocan Lake looking south, with the village of New Denver on the left
and Valhalla Provincial Park on the right.*

This is a story of a 25-year-long struggle by an active community to increase local control of forestry. From my perspective, the story begins in 1974, a year after I had immigrated to Canada from Seattle. A friend, Frans Braal, approached me to work with a number of other local residents on a study of forest management in the Slocan Valley of British Columbia. The Slocan Valley Community Forest Management Project was a grass roots study led by a steering committee of which Frans was a member. Twelve local residents and six local consultants with varied backgrounds worked for the committee. My responsibilities as part of the study team focused on economic aspects of the project, but also initially included helping to plan the work of the study team.

The 1974 final report of the Slocan Valley Community Forest Management Project contained numerous detailed findings, including the fact that most of the

Slocan Valley was totally committed to industry and was grossly over committed ecologically. The Slocan Valley economy was based on a "single user" (the forest company operating in the area), which made local forest management initiatives "next to impossible" and tied the economic future of the valley to an external marketing system. Local resources were being overused for the single purpose of producing wood fiber at the expense of water, soil, fish, wildlife, and other uses.

The recommendations of the study team focused on positive solutions to these problems. They included setting up a resource committee of local residents and government agency representatives, with responsibility for its own budget, to oversee resource management. The team advocated that for an initial period of five years, the provincial government should reinvest local stumpage revenues (fees the government charges companies for the right to log publicly owned land) into local resource management. Recommendations also included hiring a local resource manager and multidisciplinary team to prepare resource plans from existing data and on-site evaluations and recalculate the allowable annual cut of trees in the valley on a drainage-by-drainage basis.

The study team recommended a number of new initiatives, such as providing a system of "rural wood lots" for local residents to manage as small tree farms, establishing a 50,000 hectare (125,000 acre) Valhalla Provincial Park on the west side of Slocan Lake, and setting up small processing plants to produce more value from local forest products. Recommended policy changes included requiring sawmills to burn wood waste as fuel to dry lumber and increasing the price of wood chips that the government-owned pulp mill in the nearby community of Castlegar purchased from Slocan Forest Products, the primary forest licensee in the Slocan Valley. During the late 1970s, the BC government attempted two facilitated planning exercises involving government ministries and concerned citizens. The primary focus of both processes was on forestry and the need for additional protected areas. However, the government continued to maintain the status quo.

During the early 1980s, the provincial government stepped up its planning efforts in the Slocan Valley and conducted a comprehensive planning process for the watershed. Government agencies and consultants conducted technical studies on recreation, demographics, tourism, mineral resources, wildlife, air/water quality, heritage resources, agriculture, economic opportunities, and community profiles. The government held a series of public meetings in June 1981, and based on this work, regional district and provincial government planners worked together on the development of a fairly balanced plan for the Slocan Valley.

This planning process dragged on for four years. Towards the end, a "Can-the-Plan" movement surfaced in opposition to the plan. People who had a stake in the forest industry and rural residents who did not want any land-use regulations on their private property led the opposition. The planners and politicians attempted to "compromise" the plan in response to the Can-the-Plan criticisms. As a result, the final plan dropped key environmental provisions, and environmental activists ended up opposing it.

This experience showed that planning processes must move quickly. Twelve to eighteen months is long enough to incorporate public input, conduct the necessary research and analysis of alternatives, and prepare draft and final plans. When the planning process drags on longer than that, information in the plan often becomes dated and staff and members of the public run out of energy to respond to minority efforts to sabotage the plan.

For 25 years, successive provincial governments have rejected most of the recommendations of the Slocan Valley Community Forest Management Project, with the important exception of the Valhalla Provincial Park, which a Social Credit government created in 1983. It is interesting that Bob Williams, an urban planner by profession and a top-ranking minister in the NDP government during the early 1970s advocated increased community control of local resource management before he became a minister and prior to the 1974 Slocan Community Forest Management Project. However, during his tenure as a minister in the NDP government, Williams rejected the project's key recommendations. Then, after the NDP was voted out of power, he used the project's final report in his classes at the UBC School of Community and Regional Planning. At about the same time, in an address to a meeting at UBC of regional district directors from across the province, Williams said that his biggest regret was not implementing the Slocan Valley community forestry recommendations when he was minister.

In 1988, support for replacing clearcutting with selection logging in the main Slocan Valley corridor and its domestic watersheds became so widespread that all three village councils in the valley, as well as the Regional District of Central Kootenay, passed resolutions calling for an end to clearcutting. Despite this unanimous input from the local communities, the BC government allowed the clearcutting to continue.

In 1990, despite widespread protests, the provincial government refused to properly evaluate the sustainability of the wood chip supply and approved expanding the Celgar pulp mill in nearby Castlegar to three times its former size. At that time, the Chinese government was part owner of the pulp mill. According to information obtained by the Valhalla Society from the Chinese embassy, the BC government agreed to allow the proposed expansion before the review committee had completed its deliberations. The government subsequently invested about $88 million in infrastructure for the pulp mill expansion, including a major bridge across the Columbia River in Castlegar and improvements to Highway 6, which runs through the Slocan Valley. The expanded pulp mill put increased demand on logging in the area and chip truck traffic through the valley.

The NDP party was returned to power in British Columbia on October 17, 1991 but the new government continued to reject the recommendations from the 1974 Slocan Valley Community Forest Management Project and subsequent public input. However, the NDP government that was elected in 1991 realized that something had to be done to end the "war in the woods" between environmentalists and the forest industry. In attempting to do this, the government established the

Ecologically responsible partial cutting in an interior Douglas fir forest, much preferable to extensive clearcut logging (for example of clearcut logging see photo on page 36).

Commission on Resources and Environment (CORE). CORE focused on the hot spots of the province – Vancouver Island, the Kootenays, and the Caribou-Chilcotin. CORE hired a large staff of planners and process facilitators to conduct a resource-use planning process in each of these three regions. This planning process was designed to end the "war in the woods" by involving multistakeholder interests in determining which areas needed to be protected and which areas would remain available for resource extraction. In addition, CORE decided to conduct a pilot local planning project in the Slocan Valley. Over the next three years, 1992 to 1994, environmental activists were overwhelmed by the amount of unpaid work and time these processes required.

During April 1993, shortly after the Kootenay CORE planning process started, the BC government announced its decision to log approximately two-thirds of the Clayoquot Sound area. This decision was totally unacceptable to the BC and Canadian environmental movements, and many environmental groups resigned as members of the regional CORE planning groups. The government's Clayoquot Sound decision caused the largest civil disobedience action in Canadian history. Over 10,000 people visited the Clayoquot Protection Peace Camp and more than 932 were arrested. In response, Canadian governments committed $47.1 million to fund public relations for BC's transnational logging companies (MacIsaac 1994).

The ongoing protests at Clayoquot Sound made it extremely difficult for environmental groups to continue their involvement in the CORE planning processes. Having resigned as members of the regional CORE planning groups, the environmental groups were in the awkward position of observing the regional planning meetings from the back of the room and requesting permission to make presentations to the remaining CORE members.

During 1994, CORE produced regional land-use plans for Vancouver Island in February and for the Kootenays in October. One of the most important elements in each of these regional land-use plans was a system for establishing protected areas. The provincial government had adopted the target of setting aside twelve percent of the provincial land base for protected areas in each of the province's regions, as recommended by the Bruntland Commission. CORE's plans specified new parks in each region to increase the total protected area to twelve percent. Other recommendations in the CORE land-use plans included special management areas that define priorities for protecting wildlife habitat, scenic areas, and domestic watersheds. Other areas were designated for "enhanced" resource extraction to encourage industrial forestry.

The West Kootenay Land Use Plan provided protection for the proposed White Grizzly Wilderness area, which is partly within the Slocan Valley. The plan confirmed the continued protection of Kokanee Glacier and Valhalla provincial parks and designated a special management area for most of the main Slocan Valley corridor. However, the Ministry of Forests has largely ignored the provisions for special management. Clearcut logging practices continue to dominate in BC's forests to this day, and the BC provincial government again rejected the recommendations made in the 1974 Slocan Community Forest Management Project calling for increased community control of logging, which CORE also recommended.

The local Slocan Valley CORE planning project addressed the issue of special management in more detail. Provincial ministries, led by the Ministry of Forests, drafted maps and plans. The Silva Forest Foundation had for many years been busy working on an ecosystem-based plan. In contrast to the Silva plan, the government's plan preserved the status quo. Like the regional CORE planning processes, the local planning process required a huge amount of unpaid time and effort from the table participants. Participating in both regional and local processes simultaneously was particularly time consuming.

After Corky Evans was elected an NDP Member of the Legislative Assembly (MLA) in 1991, he distanced himself from the 1974 report he had produced as coordinator of the Slocan Valley Community Forest Management Project. Even though Evans is presently a Minister in the cabinet,[1] the NDP government has continued to reject most of the recommendations of his 1974 report. Why did two ministers of the NDP government fail to implement changes they claimed to support? The answer to this lies in the dynamics of politics in British Columbia. First of all, the International Woodworkers of America (IWA) union has had a strong influence on the policies of the NDP government in BC. The IWA has consistently supported the status quo in forestry in order to keep union members working

---

1: In BC, the cabinet is the highest level of legislative and executive decision making.

and maintain their wage levels. The union has opposed most changes in the industry and blamed the loss of logging and sawmilling jobs on the "alienation" of forest land to parks, municipal expansion, and other forms of development, rather than on the rapidly increasing technology in sawmills and logging operations.

In effect, the alliance between the IWA, the forest industry, and the BC provincial government has remained strong. In some ways, control of the economic aspects of the forest industry by this alliance is similar to the mafia control of many economic activities during the 1920s and 30s in the United States where union and commercial/industrial interests were closely connected to mafia control and influence. Although the tactics of the BC alliance have not included the violent practices commonly employed by the mafia in the US, the BC alliance has operated with the additional benefit of stronger support from government.

In BC the wages of IWA members are higher than wages for similar work in the US and elsewhere. The economic situation of forestry workers in BC is even more tenuous now because a combination of factors – increased automation, the necessary reduction in the rate of logging due to overcutting, and a growing public awareness that other values are more important than timber production. Other important values derived from forests include maintaining a high quality of life for local residents, preserving natural scenery, preserving biological diversity, and providing reliable domestic water supplies. Although a growing majority of citizens here in BC also prize these values, governments here have resisted changes that would significantly reduce overcutting and clearcutting. Regulations contained in the new BC Forest Practices Code support the status quo by continuing to allow ecologically unsustainable rates of logging and the choice of clearcutting over selective logging, protection of wildlife habitat, and other important environmental issues.

The rate of logging in national forests in the Pacific northwest states has declined by 47 percent since 1991, when the US Supreme Court ruled that the rate of logging violated US laws protecting endangered species (e.g., the spotted owl). This change in forest management has not yet reached Canada, partly due to the lack of national or provincial endangered species legislation, but also due to the strong alliance between the provincial governments, the IWA, and industry, and the collective influence these organizations have on our elected representatives in the provincial government.

In 1995, I developed an economic transition strategy for the Slocan Valley (Copeland 1995) that identified value-added opportunities and called for a significant reduction of the allowable annual cut (AAC). The AAC is the average amount of logging per year that the provincial government allows. BC's Chief Forester determines the AAC for each forest district in the province. In BC, allowable annual cuts have exceeded the amount of logging that is sustainable over a long period of time. The Silva ecosystem-based plan for the Slocan Valley calls for an eventual 72 percent reduction in the AAC.

Among other things, the transition strategy advocated an increase in small-business timber sales. Most of the AAC is allocated to the large forest tenure holders, but small logging contractors receive a limited percentage of the cut. The tendency of the Ministry of Forests has been to make these small-business allocations in some of the most controversial areas such as Perry's Ridge in the Slocan Valley. Increasing small-business sales would help to reduce the control over logging by large companies and increase the direct involvement of smaller contractors and community-based operations.

BC has a local wood lot program that allows land owners to manage small amounts of adjacent crown forest land as wood lots. Increasing local wood lots would have effects similar to increasing small-business sales. From a community-based perspective, increasing the amount of land in wood lots makes even more sense because license holders live adjacent to the wood lots and will therefore remain involved over the long run.

Developing a log yard in the Slocan Valley would also bring economic benefits to the area and support value-added industries. BC has only one log yard now, which is located in Vernon. A yard log is a place where logs harvested under the direct supervision of the Ministry of Forests are sorted by species and quality and offered for sale to the public. Buyers of this wood have included small companies that are looking for specific types of wood for their value-added operations. Sales from the successful log yard in Vernon have generated an average of $40 per cubic meter more than the average stumpage fees in the area. The log yard has meant increased returns to the public from forest management. Logging under this program has also tended to consist of various types of selective cutting, which is considered to be more benign environmentally compared to clearcutting, the dominant type of logging practiced by the larger companies.

At present, loggers on privately owned land are exempt from the requirements of the *Forest Practices Code*. Management of private land logging would require owners of private land to adhere to the same standards specified in the Code for logging in public forests.

Other economic strategies include establishing a forest restoration program and a tree nursery for the Slocan Valley and hiring a resident forester. An accelerated forest restoration program would reduce the backlog of non-sufficiently restocked (NSR) sites throughout BC. Most NSR sites have not been sufficiently replanted to function as forests. Trees for the forest restoration program could be started in a tree nursery located in the Slocan Valley, which would provide opportunities for additional local employment. A resident forester who is an employee of the Ministry of Forests could also be directly accountable to the local community. The forester would be responsible for ensuring that all logging in the area meets the requirements of the ecosystem-based plan.

Setting up a differential stumpage system based on value added and the ecological soundness of logging practices would benefit the local economy and protect local forest resources. Operators who produce higher values from timber harvested and who log according to the highest ecological standards would pay lower stumpage fees. Operators who produce less value added and who continue to practice clearcutting would pay higher fees.

Increasing support and services from government, banks, and credit unions to small business operators would partly alleviate the disadvantage of smaller operators relative to the massive subsidies and loans that larger forest companies have received. Companies that add value to local products should also receive additional support. This is especially important for local producers of high-value wood products, such as log and timber frame homes, furniture, and windows and doors, from wood which is harvested locally.

The economic transition strategy for the Slocan Valley included an ecolabeling and certification program that would draw consumers' attention to local products that meet environmental standards. The Silva Forest Foundation is seeking this kind of certification from the Forest Stewardship Council (FSC). Under this program, those certified will be able to label forest products which meet the stringent standards of the FSC for wood that has been harvested according to ecologically sustainable standards.

The strategy advocated fostering regional wood products networks and industry-community partnerships and retraining assistance for forest workers. It also identified specific ways to increase economic diversification in the Slocan Valley. These included completing the system of protected areas, accelerating the enhancement of protected areas, establishing a local interpretive center in the Slocan Valley, fostering small business development, encouraging the wildcrafting industry and the practice of ecological stewardship, and increasing import substitution.

Protected areas are one of the most important infrastructure components for the growing ecotourism industry. Completing the system of protected areas could include expanding provincial parks in key areas: for example, adding the White Grizzly Trail, the upper part of the Whitewater Creek drainage, and an access corridor to the White Grizzly trailhead. These additions would provide better access to the new Goat Range Provincial Park.

Accelerating the enhancement of protected areas could include expanding the hiking trail system within provincial parks and encouraging appropriate tourism development outside parks. There is also an excellent opportunity for continuing the development of the rail-to-trail conversion program in the Slocan Valley. A local interpretive center in the Slocan Valley could focus on the outstanding natural features and the diverse culture of the area. Cultural interpretation could include the turn-of-the-century mining era, the Japanese internment during World War II, and the Doukabor settlement.

In addition to the development of small businesses in the forest industry, there are other opportunities for small business development in ecotourism, support services for the growing film-making sector, services for retirees, the growing high-tech industry, and home-based consulting activities. The wildcrafting industry and ecological stewardship also offer opportunities. Mushroom harvesting, for example, has been a lucrative seasonal occupation for many people in the valley.

Popular Lake in the White Grizzly (Goat Range) Provincial Park.

Government could support this industry by protecting important mushroom harvesting habitats. In the area of import substitution, there is considerable potential in the Slocan Valley for increasing agricultural production and environmentally benign sources of energy such as small hydroelectric projects.

These elements of an economic transition strategy for the Slocan Valley became part of the Silva Forest Foundation's comprehensive ecosystem-based plan (Silva Forest Foundation 1996). During economic transition, it is important to integrate all the recommendations as a package of interrelated improvements. This approach constitutes true integrated resource management. Integrated resource management is the best way to achieve optimum ecologically sustainable use of natural and human resources and to meet the challenge of implementing ecological economics.

A recent poll conducted by Angus Reid indicated that 75 percent of Slocan Valley residents support a change to this more advanced form of resource management based on ecosystem-based landscape planning. Ecosystem-based planning "focuses first on what to leave alone and then on what can be taken without causing damage to ecosystem functioning" (Silva Forest Foundation 1996). It recognizes that ecosystems are "not static and unchanging" and that forests are interconnected, interdependent clusters of ecosystems. Understanding that a "forest ecosystem is a continuum through time and space" reinforces the wisdom that what we do to one part of the forest we do to all parts of the forests.

An ecosystem-based approach is different from the traditional way of conduct-

Grant Copeland

ing business. Traditional economic development has responded primarily to the demands of the marketplace and is motivated by the need to maximize returns on investment and profitability. Management consultants often describe their approach as "market driven." This approach omits most ecological considerations since market-driven equations do not factor in animals and the nonhuman rest of nature. Traditional economic development has paid little attention to ecological sustainability (even as it affects humans) or the needs of local communities. The globalization of the economy is a gigantic extension of this traditional approach to economic development and production. Only the scale and efficiency has changed.

The Silva Forest Foundation's ecosystem-based landscape plan for the Slocan River Watershed contains a detailed scientific rationale (Silva Forest Foundation 1996) that includes a number of points. In the first place, the Silva Plan advocates maintaining fully functioning ecosystems of all sizes over the long run. This is based on the principle that all parts of ecosystems are important to the interconnected web of life and therefore it is essential to keep all parts functioning over the long run. Eliminating one or more parts poses a risk of losing the entire ecosystem.

The plan advocates balanced use of ecosystems. Balanced use means that all ecosystem users have a role in determining the uses of forests. This concept requires a major shift from past and present forest practices, which produced huge benefits for those involved in the extraction of timber but paid little attention to other users of the forests. These include, among others, domestic water users, those who enjoy intact viewscapes, recreationalists, and tourism operators.

The Silva Plan also calls for community control of the planning and use of local forest landscapes. This is based on the principle that local people care the most about the environment in which they live and from which their children and future generations will benefit.

The Silva Plan follows the precautionary principle, which means do not log when there is the possibility of unacceptable risk. It also specifies how to achieve the necessary shift from conventional timber mismanagement (e.g., clearcutting) to ecologically responsible timber management (e.g., carefully planned selection logging). It calls for the establishment of a community forest board, composed of community-based interests, to plan and carry out ecologically responsible forest use within the Slocan River watershed. This recommendation is based on the principle of community control.

The plan advocates establishing a log sorting yard and an open log market. This would eliminate, or at least significantly reduce, the tendency of government to favor and subsidize large forest tenures, because the larger companies would be forced to pay the same price for this wood as smaller operators. This would also improve access to the wood by local value-added producers.

Finally, the plan recommends ecosystem-based certification of wood and other products produced in the Slocan Valley and expanded production of value-added products. As well as increasing the value of exports from the area, this would benefit the local community by increasing employment opportunities.

The Silva Forest Foundation's detailed maps of the Slocan Valley identify areas suitable for timber extraction. The foundation's estimate of an ecosystem-based allowable annual cut indicates that logging activities would eventually need to be reduced by at least 72 percent from current levels. However, the application of a more labor-intensive, ecosystem-based logging and silvicultural system could potentially be combined with increased value-added employment to offset some of the jobs lost from reducing the AAC (Silva Forest Foundation 1996).

Despite the poll indicating that three-quarters of Slocan Valley residents support Silva's ecosystem-based plan, the present provincial government has consistently failed to implement the plan's key recommendations. Conventional logging is now moving from the remote drainages in the Slocan Valley watershed that few people see into the highly visible domestic watersheds and viewscapes of the valley. Over the past ten years, conventional logging of these more visible areas has caused widespread protest. Local residents have written hundreds of letters objecting to the way government has been managing the forests of the Slocan Valley. Over 100 people have been arrested for resisting the logging of domestic watersheds in the valley, at Bonanza Creek in the small community of Hills north of the village of New Denver, on New Denver Flats above the village, at Hasty Creek on Red Mountain south of the village of Silverton, and on Perry's Ridge near Winlaw in the southern part of Slocan Valley.

On Perry's Ridge alone, the government has squandered over $2 million pushing road construction and funding its bogus planning process, along with attendant lawsuits, police, judges, court clerks, and injunctions. By contrast, the government has refused to provide the necessary funds to conduct the terrain and ecosystem studies that its own experts have urged.

Instead of accepting Silva's ecosystem-based plan, the government has set up local area planning groups (LRUPs) which are heavily biased in favor of logging industry representatives and Ministry of Forests staff. The effect of this has been to maintain the status quo supply of timber to Slocan Forest Products (the company which has the license to log most of the valley) at the expense of the much-needed transition to community and ecosystem-based development.

Slocan Forest Products (SFP) has become the largest sawmilling company in Canada. Since 1978, when the company was incorporated, SFP has grown from a single sawmilling and logging operation in the Slocan Valley to owning eight other sawmills, two pulp mills, and two plywood plants in other areas of British Columbia. In 1993, the company employed only 0.55 persons per 1,000 cubic meters of wood cut and cut nearly three million cubic meters (Copeland 1995). According to the company's financial statements, its net profit reached nearly $100 million in 1994. This profit was in excess of the $58 million in stumpage SFP paid to government that year for wood harvested and the services the Ministry of Forests rendered in relation to the company's logging operations. According to a recent article in the Vancouver Sun, SFP is leading all forestry companies with a 41

Arrests at Bonanza Creek near the community of Hills, Slocan Valley.

Citizens protesting on Perry Ridge near Winlaw, Slocan Valley.

percent return on investment in 1999.

These figures indicate that both the provincial government and SFP realize substantial short-term cash flow from the company's operations at the expense of unaccounted environmental costs and foregone potential revenues from increasing the value added through secondary processing of wood products. Expenses not included in the government's accounting include widespread damage to domestic water supplies, siltation of downstream fish habitat, property diverted by logging roads and lost to landslides that originate in clearcuts, deterioration of visual quality and property values, and reduction in the overall quality of life of valley residents.

Thus far, despite over 25 years of active community involvement, the provincial government has avoided transition to a more diversified and more community-based economy. This has been extremely frustrating to concerned local citizens who have worked for changes. The only encouraging signs are that younger people and newcomers to the valley have been getting more involved in the struggle.

The Slocan Valley experience is not unique in BC. Many other communities are demanding a change to the current forest tenure and management system. Increasingly, the provincial government has been challenged to provide more community control of forest practices. Some 90 communities have applied for community tree farm licenses or other forms of tenure that provide increased local control of logging. This is primarily because these communities now realize that the long-term health of ecosystems forms the basis for economic and community stability.

The University of Victoria has developed a legislative solution in the form of the Community Forest Trust Act (Burda, Curran, Gale and M'Gonigle 1997). This proposal offers unique mechanisms for implementing ecosystem-based community forestry over time as communities prepare for this new responsibility and are willing to develop the capacities needed to take it on. Some communities, such as the Slocan Valley, are already well prepared, in part because professionals living in the valley have developed an ecosystem-based plan that could serve as a model for the future.

Under the proposed Community Forest Trust Act, the government could not abolish, replace, or interfere with any existing tenures on trust lands. Community-based management would coexist with existing tenures. Any changes to the condition of existing tenures would be based on scientific assessments of what is necessary for sustained forest management. Implementation would take place through an inclusive, local, democratic process.

In my own view, British Columbians should seek an immediate province-wide reduction of at least 50 percent in the AAC to bring it more in line with the sustainable limits of ecosystem-based forestry. In addition, most taxpayers would probably want to eliminate, or at least significantly reduce, perverse subsidies to the forest industry once they learn how much the forest industry has been costing them (estimated in Chapter 15). And the provincial government could offer a

Herb Hammond

Above:
Clearcut in the
Memphis Creek water-
shed, Slocan Valley.

Right:
Section of Hwy 6
completely washed out
by Memphis Creek
landslide, caused by
clearcutting and road-
building in the
photo above.

Grant Copeland

rapid shift to community-based forestry, which is now in popular demand, as an option to communities. In the US, the overall economy has benefited from a Supreme Court order for a similar 47 percent reduction in logging within the national forests of Washington and Oregon. As a result of several decades of sustained political procrastination, BC now needs similar drastic measures. It would have been far easier to make the transition to ecosystem-based, community forestry 25 years ago when it was recommended by the Slocan Community Forest Management Project. It is late, but not too late to do it now.

Confrontation over forestry practices is increasing across the province. It is clearly time to make changes that are essential from an ecosystem-based point of view. Without these changes, the war-in-the-woods, which is far from over, will likely continue to escalate in the form of more blockades, lawsuits, and boycotts of wood products exported from the province. Unless we are prepared to change what we are doing in managing forests, the focus of economic development will remain on the traditional resource-extraction industries, and we will continue to ignore the needs of the more promising up-and-coming economic sectors. As a result, BC's high taxes will probably continue to discourage investment and jobs in the more promising economic sectors.

Chapter 5

RETALLACK RESORT:
DEVELOPING WITH A LIGHT TOUCH

Pete Leontowicz has been involved in mining exploration and development since he served in the Canadian Navy during World War II. He has worked in many of the major mines in the Slocan Camp, which encompasses the lake-front villages of New Denver and Silverton, Slocan City, and the ghost towns of Retallack, Sandon, and Cody. Rich silver deposits were discovered in the 1890s, and shortly thereafter, two railroad companies competed for the lucrative shipping of ore to smelters in the United States. The Slocan Camp was the most important producer of silver in the British Empire during World War I. Depletion of the more accessible ore bodies and declining markets led to the end of this Silvery Slocan era, and the last operating mine in Sandon finally closed in 1990. In the Slocan Valley, the mining era had effectively come to an end.

Nevertheless, Pete has remained optimistic that there is still plenty of ore in the area, and although well into his retirement years, he continued to prospect. However, during the summer of 1991, motivated by the decline in mining activities in the area and low silver prices, Pete and his son John came up with the idea of developing a small resort as a way to diversify their activities and use their extensive mining properties located around the ghost town of Retallack between New Denver and Kaslo.

Since for eight years I had been involved in setting up and operating Valhalla Mountain Touring, a local ski touring company, and was known as a planning consultant, the Leontowicz family approached me for advice. We worked together on a conceptual plan for a small-scale, all-season resort featuring guided snowcat skiing during the winter, guided ecotours in the summer and early fall, and other group activities such as weddings and corporate seminars during the off-season periods.

From the beginning, the plan called for community control of the project. People could earn shares in exchange for barter work and cash. Shareholders could own more than one share, but each shareholder would have only one vote regardless of the number of shares owned. Although most shareholders of the company live in the local community, investors who were in the process of moving into the community or living outside the community bought a large number of shares for cash. The purpose of one vote per shareholder was to maintain local control of the corporation.

The initial group of shareholders obtained unanimous early support for the proposed project from the MLA representing the valley, the Regional District, and all four village governments in the area, as well as local chambers of commerce and the Valhalla Society, the leading environmental group in the area. The Minister of Small Business, Tourism and Culture also gave the project strong support. During the fall of 1991, the organizers presented the concept, along with letters from the project's high-profile supporters, to a meeting of government officials in Nelson to secure the necessary land-use permits for the resort's proposed summer and winter activities.

Heavy timber-frame construction and granite fireplace of Retallack Lodge are reminiscent of the historic Silvery Slocan mining era.

The project received an exploration permit in 1993. The company purchased a snowcat, snowmobile, and other equipment and began to investigate, on-the-ground, the feasibility of developing the proposed resort.

At about this time, the government declared a moratorium on issuing commercial back-country recreation (CBR) permits while it worked on revising its CBR policy. This meant that there was no policy for commercial recreation activities on crown land and that all proposed CBR proposals were put on hold. The directors of Retallack Resort focused on lobbying the provincial government in Victoria to develop the policy and/or issue an operating permit. This required constant phone calls and numerous trips to the provincial capital in Victoria to lobby ministers and ministry staff, plus many other trips to Nelson and Cranbrook government offices.

Without a definitive CBR policy, it was difficult to obtain any support from the multiple agencies involved in approving crown land-use permits, even though they

Snowboarder in gladed area, Retallack Alpine Adventures.

all indicated support in principle for our proposed project. These agencies included the BC Lands and the Fish and Wildlife branches of the Ministry of Environment, the Ministry of Forests, and the Ministry of Small Business, Tourism and Culture. Jurisdictional authorities overlapped and were not well defined, particularly between the Ministry of Environment and Ministry of Forests. The Ministry of Tourism has little staffing or influence in the provincial government relative to the dominant roles of the Ministries of Forests and Environment.

In 1996 Retallack Alpine Adventures finally received a permit for winter snowcat operations, five years after we applied for it. Three years later in 1999, the government issued a permit for summer ecotourism operations. During these years when we were working on obtaining operational permits, another snowcat operator commenced operations in the same area without the required permit. To its credit, BC lands shut down this illegal operation and confiscated its snowcat.

After receiving the CBR permit for snowcat skiing activities, the company had to acquire more permits required by other government agencies, the key one being permission to develop winter snowcat trails and glade ski runs. In a meeting with Ministry of Forests and Slocan Forest Products, the company that held most of the logging rights within the resort's operating area, ministry officials told us we had to develop a five-year forest development plan to meet the requirements of the new Forest Practices Code. This required spending tens of thousands of dollars for engineering and other expertise. Nearly a year after receiving our five-year plan, the Ministry of Forests informed us that the plan was not necessary and that we would have to work out our development plans with the licensee Slocan Forest Products (SFP). The inappropriate and unnecessary demands of the Ministry of Forests had wasted tens of thousands of dollars of the company's funds and several months of hard work by the resort's directors.

Working out a forest development plan with Slocan Forest Products (SFP) has been a far from easy process because the company's and the Ministry of Forests' preferred method of logging is clearcutting, which involves the least short-term logging costs. Our plans called for selective logging of the areas that SFP proposed to clearcut, plus the glading (clean up) of ski runs in higher elevation terrain above the operable timber harvesting terrain. We repeatedly presented the merits of our plans to both the Ministry of Forests and Slocan Forest Products. Although, to its credit, SFP was willing to modify its plans, the Ministry of Forests did not want to deviate from the approved plans to clearcut. We protested that the clearcut logging would open up additional avalanche start zones within our operating area and in fact, SFP agreed to reduce the size of clearcuts and undertake a small proportion of selective logging, but most of SFP's clearcutting went ahead as planned with the sanction of the Ministry of Forests.

Some of SFP's logging contractors and one of its field supervisors understood that selective logging would be much better for our planned ski activities. One of the lead fallers was a skier who had worked on glading programs for Canadian Mountain Holidays, the world's largest helicopter skiing company. He and the logging contractor that employed him were willing to modify their plans to accommodate our concerns, but the Ministry of Forests would not allow the change, and SFP was also reluctant to pay the higher costs of selection logging. The next winter, as we predicted, the clearcut logging created another major avalanche hazard directly above the main access road to Jackson Basin, where most of the resort's snowcat skiing was planned.

In total, Retallack Resort spent over $200,000 in time and money over a six-year period to secure permits to begin developing the resort. This process included several reiterations of the required management plan and the five-year forest development plan. With the absence of either a model management plan or forest development plan or clear directions from government, we had to second guess what the Lands Branch and the Ministry of Forests wanted.

After the permit was issued for winter snowcat operations, the Regional District of Central Kootenay issued a building permit at a cost of $9,000 for the construction of a 24-bed lodge. The lodge features heavy timber framing reminiscent of the Silvery Slocan mining era and is embellished with details and colors used in Tibetan mountain architecture. The company commissioned detailed structural, mechanical, and sprinkler engineering of the lodge. During April of 1996, with snow still on the site, construction of the lodge commenced.

During construction, the building inspector demanded numerous structural, mechanical and other changes that ended up costing approximately $60,000 extra, according to our structural and mechanical engineers. These included three sets of unattractive double steel fire doors, despite the small size of the building and the complete sprinkler fire protection system; expensive fire door hardware that the

Retallack Lodge under construction.

building inspector did not require initially; increasing the floor joist design from 60 to 100 pounds per square foot; providing double 5/8-inch gyprock on the ceilings directly above the sprinklers; oversizing the interior plumbing pipes; installing sprinklers in the walk-in freezer and closed-off attic; double-insulated steel doors to cover plumbing cleanouts and the hydronic heating manifolds; rebuilding the kitchen vent stack, which ended up costing about $20,000, more than all of the kitchen equipment, and many other requirements. These overrun costs would have been even higher had the company not eventually challenged the building inspector and filed an appeal with the administrator of the Regional District. To his credit, the administrator immediately instructed his chief building inspector to investigate our concerns, and the chief inspector quickly approved the project. The building inspector responsible is no longer employed by the regional district, but nevertheless the cost overrun represented a huge waste of the company's limited development funds.

It took another year and approximately $6,000 to get a separate permit and custom engineering for the construction of the planned hot tub, an important amenity which will cost less than $15,000 to install. Commercial hot tubs are common in resorts and hotels and should not be that difficult to engineer and approve.

From the company's perspective, all of these extra costs, which total at least $75,000, or about nine percent of the estimated cost of construction for the building, and at least half of the $200,000 spent on obtaining operating permits could have been much better spent on important items such as more glading of ski runs, more effective marketing, construction of the hot tub and a snowcat garage, and a good audio-visual system for the lodge. From the resort's perspective, the building permit process provided no benefits to the company or its clients because the resort's team of professional architects and engineers were responsible for ensuring the quality and safety of the actual construction. Visitors and clients, competitors, and even the Regional District's chief building inspector have consistently complemented the resort for the quality and design of its lodge.

During the process of developing a management plan and subsequent five-year forest development plan, the resort discovered that BC's new Forest Practices Code would make some of the planned snowcat access roads prohibitively expensive to develop. This discovery, plus the Valhalla Society's expression of concern about some aspects of the development, led the resort to change its plans substantially. These changes included relocating or eliminating some of the proposed snowcat access routes. On balance, these changes represented improvements in meeting public concerns about environmental, social, and economic factors associated with the development. Some of the changes were also better for the company. However, the Valhalla Society also demanded other changes, including a complete repudiation and costly revision of the forest development plan. Near the end of 1995, the Society published and widely distributed a six page newsletter advocating additional changes to the company's plans (Valhalla Society 1995). Less than half a page of this newsletter focused on the problem of SFP's clearcutting in the area. The remainder of the newsletter addressed the Society's opinions regarding problems posed by the development of the resort.

The resort's five-year forest development plan provided more details on proposed tree cutting and road location than the level of detail which had been provided by the much larger logging company for its tenure areas in the Slocan Valley. For example, the resort's plan explained in considerable detail the proposed cutting prescriptions and provided aerial photographs in addition to topographic maps of the proposed ski area development. Five-year operating plans which had been submitted by the large forest companies often did not even indicate silvicultural prescriptions.

The resort refused to make these additional changes because to do so would have extended the development period by many months, and there is a limit to the amount of time and money a company can afford to spend on the planning process. For the Retallack Resort project, these costs were already more than the company could afford and more than much larger developments had been required to spend. The planning stage for the resort had already lasted more than five years, and to finance this work the company had to cancel important improvements it had planned to make. These extra costs and cancellations further delayed the start up of operations. For these reasons, the directors of the company decided that the additional changes that the Valhalla Society advocated were unrealistic. Subsequently, I resigned as a director of the society, which I had helped to found more than 20 years earlier.

During the first two years of operation, 1996 to 1998, the resort generated a substantial operating loss which the company had to cover through additional shareholder loans. Fortunately, the operation came close to breaking even during the third winter season. As of June 1999, eight years after the incorporation of the company, the resort had not generated any return on its shareholders' investment. No return is expected for at least another two to three years. None of the directors or shareholders have been paid for their work on behalf of the company.

The company was unable to secure financing from local banks and credit unions, but the Business Development Bank of Canada and Community Futures in Nelson provided loans for about a third of the capital requirements. Approximately two-thirds of the capital requirements had to be raised by issuing shares in return for cash and barter services.

Although it will take three to four years of operation before Retallack Resort reaches a break-even point, this is not unusual for similar resort developments. Small economic development projects seldom realize profits during their formative years. Snowcat skiing operators in the area have reported that they did not show a profit until at least the fifth year of operation.

It is also very difficult for small economic development projects such as Retallack Resort to achieve success without community support. In the Retallack Resort experience, strong initial community support was followed by mixed support from several elements of the community. Although the Valhalla Society supported the project in the beginning, later the Society resisted the development of the project and organized community members to speak out against it at public meetings.

Although local snowmobile users had little objection to the project at first, rapid technological improvements to snowmobiles has resulted in significant increases in the use of snowmobiles, and this has caused difficulties. These difficulties are caused by tracks left by snowmobiles in the snow-covered ski terrain. These tracks provide a dangerous and extremely undesirable situation for skiers. Although most local snowmobile users support the Retallack Resort now, a few still resist efforts to divide the available terrain between snowmobilers, skiers, and snowcat skiing.

The resort currently employs 10 to 12 people during the ski season and has the potential to employ 20 to 24 workers, but the prospect of more jobs has not generated substantial support for the project from a few special interest groups in the community, including the Valhalla Society. Even other small business operators, including several tour operators who continue to work in the area without the required land-use permits, have been reluctant to support the completion of the project publicly.

In the current investment climate, local entrepreneurs are not likely to propose such a project, much less weather public resistance from influential segments of the community, difficult financial challenges, and numerous other risks. In this case, the vocal objectors and the silent members of the community who support the project but do not feel comfortable speaking out publicly in favor of it have both defaulted to the forces of the growing global economy.

Governments have failed to appreciate the value of small, local enterprises in creating jobs and diversifying the local economy. Governments have often been quick to support megaprojects such as pulp mills that employ hundreds of workers, despite devastating effects on the environment and huge public costs. While governments fail to provide effective environmental stewardship in regard to these large projects, government agencies tend to overregulate smaller projects with endless red tape and circular multiagency processes. Large companies can afford the expense of lawyers, biologists, planners, engineers, and other professional assistance that the permit-granting process requires, but small businesses find it more difficult to pay for these professional services because the expense constitutes a much higher percentage of their development and operating costs.

Most of the shareholders of Retallack Resort have sustained an optimistic belief in the project's social, economic, and environmental benefits. They still believe that the project provides a better land-use option than industrial clearcutting, that the project is an appropriate way to generate new employment in the community and diversify the local economy, and that it will eventually generate a reasonable return on their investment. But none of the people involved knew that it would take eight years to receive the required land-use permits and reach the break even point financially.

Governments tend to tax small projects excessively. Before the Retallack lodge was completed, the company received a property tax bill for $11,000. This was the consequence of an existing provincial government policy to triple property taxes on commercial developments located outside municipalities. After the lodge was completed, the property tax doubled. There is no effective appeal to this policy.

In return for its taxes, the Retallack Resort receives few services from government. The resort maintains its own access road, generates electrical and heating power from its small hydroelectric generator, and maintains its own communications, water, sewage disposal, and fire control systems. Government assistance has been limited to posting two signs on the highway and an occasional visit from the RCMP. There is no relationship between the resort's tax assessment and the services provided or its return on investment and ability to pay. For small businesses, it would help to defer their property taxes until they begin to show a return on investment. In addition to exorbitant property taxes, the corporation had to pay numerous operational assessments and fees and charges for permits. Government agencies at the provincial and regional district level are often quick to collect fees and taxes and slow to deliver services and approvals.

In order to resist the rapidly increasing economic domination by transnational corporations and the trend toward globalization of the economy, local communities need to identify what constitutes acceptable socioeconomic development. It is no longer enough to merely oppose economic development projects, especially community controlled ones. The key challenge for communities, particularly local governments and community interest groups, is to identify those projects which are relatively benign environmentally, which offer meaningful employment, and which are economically feasible, and then to actively support these projects. This process will require a reasonable amount of compromise, and not everyone will be completely satisfied with the outcome. But larger environmental and social problems are likely to result when the projects are much larger and are controlled by investors living outside the community.

**Acts of Balance
Part 3:**

QUALITY OF LIFE
AND ECONOMIC DIVERSITY

Overview

Many North American communities have developed around the activities associated with resource extraction, particularly mining, logging, and fishing. The depletion of mineral, timber, and fishery resources has precipitated severe economic recession in many of these communities, and some, like the mining towns of Sandon, Anyox, and Kitsault and the logging community of Ocean Falls, have become ghost towns. On the other hand, some local economies which have become more resilient, more diversified, and more dynamic have been able to survive shutdowns of mines or sawmills.

To a large extent, elected representatives have followed prevailing popular folk economics and assumed that economic policy planning is unnecessary. Folk economics assumes that the processing of natural resources is the center of economic development – that communities will live with resource extraction but die without it. As a result, many communities have scrambled to preserve their mining, logging and fishing activities at all costs.

Recent research has demonstrated that folk economics is incomplete and misleading. According to Tom Power, professor and chair of the Department of Economics at the University of Montana in Missoula, folk economics assumes that people can afford to live in an area only when extracting and exporting raw materials or products manufactured from them brings income into the local economy.

According to Power, two incorrect assumptions underlie this economic base model (Power 1988,1996). First, it is not true that people don't care were they live; in fact many, if not most, people are seeking higher-quality residential environments. Second, businesses have changed the economic geography across North America by locating in areas that have reliable labor supplies. These two factors tend to occur together because workers prefer to stay where they are if the living conditions are good.

During a visit to Nelson in 1993, Power explained to a large audience in the Capital Theater how much the traditional export-base model differs from actual distribution of income in Nelson. During 1992, nearly a decade after the shut-down of Nelson's sawmill and plywood manufacturing facility, timber production provided 57 percent of total income, according to the export-base model. By comparison, under Power's model, during this same year this sector provided only 15 percent of actual income and people living in Nelson earned more than half of their total income, from the production of local goods and services.

People care where they live. Because of this, and because businesses care about the location of labor supplies and markets, desirable environments have a value of their own that does not depend on the extraction potential of the landscape. As a consequence, high-quality natural environments are becoming more valuable as desirable places to live. When possible, workers tend to locate in desirable living environments. Given a choice, most people will avoid living next to clearcuts or open-pit mines.

Power makes another interesting point. Despite the high wages normally associated with extraction industries, few towns devoted to these activities are prosperous. Power's research has revealed that as a general rule, the more dependent a community is on a single industry, the more depressed it seems to be. In addition to this, extraction industries have declined in absolute numbers but, more importantly, as a percentage of the total economy. In the Pacific northwest states and in British Columbia, extraction industries provide a small percentage of both jobs and income. In the Pacific northwest states, jobs in the forest industry constituted only 3.8 percent of total jobs in 1988. Today this percentage is much lower. In 1997, the forest industry employed only 5.5 percent of total workers in British Columbia.

Power's empirical analysis shows that:

"... mining, timber, and agriculture make a much more modest contribution to local economies than is usually assumed. The ongoing transformation of local economies, including technological and market changes, has drastically reduced the relative importance of resource extraction industries. As a result, rather than being a source of economic vitality, these economic sectors are likely to cause a declining and destabilizing role in local economies of the future" (Power 1996).

A study of over 11,000 migrants and residents in 15 wilderness counties in the western US found that counties adjacent to federally designated wilderness areas grew twice as fast on average as metropolitan areas (Rudzitis and Johansen 1989). This study found that economic considerations were important variables in determining the location of only 27 percent of those interviewed. The most important reasons for locating in a wilderness county were the environmental and physical amenities, the scenery, outdoor recreation, and the pace of life. When queried about their attitudes toward development, 90 percent of recent migrants and 85 percent of long time residents felt that it was important to "keep the environment in its natural state."

According to Power, the main issue is not protecting the spotted owl, maintaining prized Steelhead fishing, or preserving old-growth trees at the expense of economic health. The main issue is ensuring economic health by avoiding needless damage to the natural environment. Maintaining the long-run economic vitality of communities requires that we not sacrifice environmental quality to the needs of declining extraction industries. Decisions that favor preservation and protection often result in net gains in employment. The relevant challenge we face is not a choice between protecting jobs and protecting the environment, but how we can best protect the long-run economic vitality of communities.

Only approximately ten percent of economic activity provides us with goods and services that are necessary for biological survival. The rest satisfies our desire for things we want but do not really need. We currently face an important challenge – to improve our wellbeing while reducing the material pressures on the environment. To do this we must abandon the emphasis on quantitative expansion of material production. Communities that take this course are able to provide a more diverse and interesting environment for recreation, sports, community services, arts and crafts, and home-based businesses, and they are relatively self-sufficient.

Healthy economies are always changing. Some sectors experience growth while others decline. Technological advances and more environmentally friendly ways to produce goods and services are positive changes. Canadian and US economies could not have modernized without many changes in the way we do things. Labor needs have changed radically from those of a hunter-gatherer economy to agrarian to industrial to the present information age. Most jobs around the world now require better training and education to deal with more complex technology, new information needs, and more sophisticated methods of production and marketing. Providing services has expanded into the largest economic sector. Responding to these and other changes requires new economic policies backed by assistance to displaced workers who are experiencing difficulty in the transition to new, different, and often more challenging employment opportunities. Instead of accepting change and working on the necessary transition, we have tended to treat each job change as a personal and social catastrophe.

Lester Thurow points out that the seven key industries of the next few decades are all "brainpower" industries: microelectronics, biotechnology, new materials industries, civilian aviation, telecommunications, robotics and machine tools, and computers and software. An important aspect of these industries is that they are "footloose" – they can locate anywhere (Thurow 1993).

A commonly heard myth about economic development and the transition to a more service-oriented, information-age economy concerns the loss of high wage jobs. However, relatively high-wage industries now form the largest components of the service economy. In the Greater Yellowstone area, 29 percent of services consist of engineering and management services and another 22 percent in health services. Together these two service sectors total 51 percent of the service economy. On average, the salaries in the service industries are 20 percent higher than average wages in all other industries (Rasker 1994). Services have become the fastest growing part of the economy in rich countries, where over half of all workers are employed in the production, storage, retrieval, or distribution of knowledge (*Economist* 1993).

The qualitative term *vitality* is a better way of describing the dynamism and diversity of economic opportunities we seek in local economies than *growth*, which is quantitative. According to economists Tom Power and Ray Rasker, people will commit significant resources to get access to preferred climates, low crime rates, recreation opportunities, low congestion, clean air and water, good schools, and cultural amenities. Power describes this another way: People get two "pay checks" as a result of choosing better residential amenities. They get a quality-of-life bonus in addition to the usual cash payment associated with productive activity. Together, the two pay checks represent the aggregate economic wellbeing and vitality of a community.

In his book *The Economic Pursuit of Quality*, Power suggests creating a better balance between the commercial and noncommercial aspects of life in our communities, along with a number of other visionary changes (Power 1988). Power suggests enriching the range of cooperative activities; constraining coercive, bureaucratic government; supporting the individual and the household within a social context; and replacing "growth" with "vitality." Other ideas focus on pursuing directly the qualities we want, shifting the scale to local and small, increasing the self-sufficiency of local communities, developing qualities and activities in place of material goods, creating good work, not more jobs, and developing a community approach to avoiding poverty.

Throughout history and across North America, the forest industry has logged at unsustainable rates. The industry has been "mining" the stock of large mature trees that grew naturally over hundreds of years. As the industry exhausts this stock of old-growth trees and begins to log the much smaller second-growth trees, the rate of logging drops significantly. Industry has called this the "fall-down effect." Several investigations of the industry, including the 1976 Pearse Commission and the 1991 Forest Resources Commission in BC, have estimated a substantial fall-down effect. Further drops in logging are inevitable as society insists that forest managers give greater attention to clean water, fish and wildlife, ecotourism, visual quality, and other values derived from forests.

In British Columbia, the government's failure to produce and implement an effective economic strategy for adjusting to the fall-down effect in the forest industry has caused widespread fear and hardship in communities. Instead of attempting to accelerate the shift of forest-industry workers to different jobs, the provincial government has delayed this transition.

Province-wide, direct and indirect public costs of the forest industry approach an estimated $10.2 billion per year or roughly $136,000 per worker. (See section on perverse subsidies in Chapter 15.) This is not the best use of tax revenue. Taxpayers' dollars can generate more employment through increased investment in growing industries such as the film industry, high technology (e.g., the production of fuel cells), and ecotourism. Because small businesses already create the bulk of sustainable, new employment, government could also be more effective by helping small businesses to create more new jobs.

A few communities have consciously or unconsciously made some positive moves towards diversifying their economies and moving away from dependence on resource extraction. The most important objective underlying these changes has been to maintain and improve quality of life in these communities. In these forward thinking and active communities, the value of protecting the environment has become more and more important to residents. Non-wage incomes from investments and retirement funds have also grown in importance.

The next three chapters describe some of the changes that have taken place in three Pacific northwest communities. Redmond, Washington, is a suburban area outside Seattle which has evolved from a small bedroom community to a leading high technology center. Smithers and Nelson are two rural BC communities which have diversified their economies and survived the transition from heavy dependence on resource extraction activities. Each of these communities places a very high value on maintaining their surrounding environment and a strong sense of community identity.

Chapter 6

REDMOND:
PLANNING FOR THE INFORMATION AGE

When I graduated from the University of Washington with a Masters degree in planning in 1969, I was hired to head up a team formed to develop a comprehensive plan for the City of Redmond. At that time, Redmond was a bedroom suburb on the outskirts of Seattle. The City of Redmond borders the north end of Lake Sammamish and the City of Kirkland to the west. From the beginning, we used a process that integrated economic and ecological planning. This approach still influences the policies contained in the Redmond Plan.

Before the team drafted any planning policies, it initiated a process that resulted in a detailed ecological analysis of the area. This analysis examined the local climate, geology, hydrology, physiography, pedology (soil science), vegetation, and wildlife. Using this data base, the team studied and mapped the intrinsic suitability of the land for different purposes and employed a system of map overlays to examine the compatibility of various proposed land uses. The Redmond Plan includes land-use policies that prohibit development within the 100-year flood plain, avoid development on steep slopes, maintain existing vegetation and wildlife, and encourage the preservation of existing agricultural uses.

Careful implementation of these ecosystem-based policies over the past 30 years has helped to protect the natural environment of the Redmond area. Most of the flood plain area remains in near natural condition, and the steep slopes visible from the town have retained their natural forest cover.

In 1969 Redmond's population numbered 11,000, but by 1987 it had grown to 30,000. By that time businesses in the city employed over 22,000 people. By then, the city had become a high technology center. Key businesses located in Redmond include Microsoft, which set up business in Redmond around 1979, and Sunstrand Data Control. Of the approximately 2,500 businesses in Redmond in 1987, only 38 employed over 100 workers and over 70 percent employed less than five. The city's emphasis was on encouraging the development of small-scale, community-based businesses. Over the last 30 years, these businesses have developed a clear track record of sustainable employment.

Redmond changed from a bedroom community where most residents commuted to work in other places within the Seattle metropolitan area to a major center of employment. By 1995, the Redmond population had increased to 40,000, and the number of jobs in the community also reached 40,000. Many workers in Redmond now commute from homes outside the city. Redmond's "beautiful setting as a desirable place in which to live, work and play" is partly responsible for

Grant Copeland

*Photo of Planning Team printed in the 1970
Redmond Optimum Land Use Plan.*

Ron McConnell

Hiker in Redmond Watershed Preserve.

Microsoft campus in Redmond, Washington.

this growth in population and employment. Visitors to the Microsoft campus are amazed by the amount of open space and the quality of the landscaping. It is more like a park than a place of business. This environment has paid great dividends to the company – several thousand millionaires have earned their fortunes at Microsoft, which today remains the world leader in computer software. For recent university graduates, Microsoft is one of the most preferred employers in the world. Average starting wages are approximately $75,000 US (Ochs 1999).

The 1970 Redmond Optimum Land Use Plan had a number of key goals or values which have remained as part of the city's subsequent land-use plans. These plans call for community identity, economic balance, social variations within the community, adequate parks and open spaces, conservation of natural resources, and public and private partnerships.

The Redmond Plan was also based on a comprehensive economic analysis of the structure of the local and regional economies. In addition to assembling quantifiable information on population, income, and employment trends, the planning team organized meetings with focus groups, business leaders, and citizen groups on community values and business development prospects. The plan incorporated information on local land ownership and land values and the supply and demand for various types of housing, as well as detailed targets for achieving a balanced mix of housing to fit the needs of different household incomes. Because these targets were solidly based on a comprehensive economic analysis, housing developers used them, and they had a significant influence on the types, location, and prices of new housing.

A policy for phased construction of sewer trunk lines and other key municipal infrastructure has allowed the City of Redmond to control development so that it did not spread too fast. This policy offered the most economical method of providing municipal services.

One interesting issue that surfaced during the process of developing the Redmond Plan was the city council's proposal to use a 880-acre parcel of municipally owned land for the development of a private aviation airport. A study of this proposal revealed that only 11 of the Redmond residents who owned airplanes would use the facility. In 1970, the appraised value of this site was $2.2 million. The study estimated that the value of the site would increase to $22 million by 1990. In addition to using valuable land, the airport would have been costly to develop, and its operation would have demanded continuous subsidies.

When the Seattle area media reported on the release of the airport study during a public council meeting, Redmond residents protested. To its credit, the council reversed its decision (the councillor who had spearheaded the project resigned). In 1997, the city developed the site as the Redmond Watershed Preserve, one of the major regional nature parks in the Seattle area.

Chapter 7

SMITHERS: WILD AND DIVERSE

Integrating the concepts of sustainable economic development and environmental management in community planning is a relatively new phenomenon in British Columbia. BC's *Municipal Act* does not require municipalities to include these subjects in official community plans. Traditionally, community plans address land-use and zoning issues and the development of municipal services such as roads and sewer and water systems. As a result, most municipal plans do not have the benefit of a scientific examination of the geology, topography, hydrology, and vegetation of the region, or a detailed analysis of the structural aspects of and trends in the regional and local economies. Because of this, policy making and decisions involved in implementing municipal plans do not deal adequately with environmental and economic concerns. Most plans do not have an environmental and economic rationale.

During 1988 and the early part of 1989, I was hired to revise the Official Community Plan and Outdoor Recreation Master Plan for the town of Smithers in northwestern BC. Smithers is located in the scenic Bulkley Valley and is flanked on the west by Hudson Bay Mountain and on the east by the Babine Mountains. The town was established as a maintenance center for the Grand Trunk Railway and sits precisely midway between Prince George and Prince Rupert. Since the turn of the century, Smithers has served as a center for mining exploration and development in northern BC. Cattle and dairy farms were developed in the Bulkley Valley and a dairy processing plant was located in Smithers. Sawmills were built to process timber harvested in the area. More recently, Smithers has become a popular tourist destination with a ski hill, world-class sports fishing, great hiking opportunities, and other forms of back-country recreation. It also provides shopping and other services for nearby First Nation communities.

Partly because of its diversity, Smithers is a vibrant place to live and work, both economically and socially. Drawn by the beauty of the area, many immigrants from Switzerland, other European countries, the United States, and across Canada have settled in the community. Some purchased rural acreage in the Bulkley Valley and have been long-time residents of the area. The population of the municipality recently exceeded the 5,000 mark and now provides its own police protection. Approximately the same number of people live in the surrounding rural area and in the nearby village of Telkwa.

Economic and social diversity are strengths of the community. Despite the broad range of incomes, ethnic heritage, religions, and strong individual beliefs, the residents of the area take collective pride in their community and have worked

Bulkley Valley farmland helps support the economic diversity of Smithers.

together to build a wide range of recreational facilities, including two golf courses, a large fairground complex, numerous well-maintained hiking trails, ball fields, tennis courts, a hockey arena, a downhill skiing facility, and even a world-class archery range. The community also worked together to build an indoor swimming pool, for which the community's own businesses and residents donated a substantial amount of the financing. A few years ago, the high school was equipped with a performing arts theater. Communities the size of Smithers rarely have all these facilities.

Because of the outstanding outdoor recreation opportunities in the area, the exceptionally beautiful rural landscape, frontage on the Bulkley River, the diverse array of community facilities, and the town's alpine architectural motif, many residents and visitors regard Smithers as one of the most desirable places to live in BC, or perhaps in North America. This quality of life is of the utmost importance to the residents of Smithers. Conservatives, liberals, farmers, loggers, railroad workers, government employees, tourism operators, and most other residents all care deeply about their community. The unusual level of commitment and involvement in community affairs reflects this concern.

During the process of updating the community plan, the planning team put together background data on various economic sectors and economic trends. This included both the "desk work" of assembling published information and the "field work" of gathering opinions from private interviews with community and business leaders and from public meetings with interest groups. The Chamber of

Commerce became involved in creating an economic development strategy through a series of weekly early-morning meetings. Analysis of all this information led to an economic development policy that eventually became part of the Smithers Official Community Plan.

Smithers Economic Development Policy

The Smithers Economic Development Policy states that, "Continued economic stability depends upon maintaining and enhancing the diversified economic components of the Smithers economy. It is the policy of Council to continue to maintain its diversified economy and moderate, manageable growth rate. . ." The Smithers Economic Development Strategy contains the following elements:

- encourage the maintenance of the community's stable government payroll, which consists primarily of provincial government employees.

- support an optimum sustainable forest industry by matching the capacity of local milling facilities to the profile of the available timber supply.

- develop secondary manufacturing and increase the value of forest products exported from the area.

- encourage the use of Smithers as a base of operations, service center, and location for training facilities for mining exploration, development, and production.

- continue providing comprehensive regional retail and wholesale sales services.

- serve as a transportation staging service center for rail, air, and highway traffic.

- develop the community's strong intrinsic tourism opportunities, which are based on the exceptional quality and diversity of the natural resources of the Bulkley Valley and the northwest region of the province.

- develop ancillary services such as more high-quality restaurants with increased ethnic diversity to meet the demands of visiting tourists and business people.

- develop recreation facilities such as a perimeter trail system, swimming pool, cross-country ski trails, and improvements to Ski Smithers.

- encourage the provincial government to develop an integrated resource-use plan which effectively recognizes the tourism industry.

- support the agricultural industry by supporting the Agricultural Land Reserve.

- provide increased opportunities for First Nations people living in the area to become involved in economic development which is appropriate to their traditional and preferred life styles.

With the exception of mining, most of the policies in the Smithers community plan contribute to a diversified economy that is relatively sustainable ecologically. There is always room to improve the environmental performance of almost any economic sector, but Smithers is far ahead of most other northern communities in setting policies that help to guide the community to ecological sustainability.

To support this approach to community planning and economic development, the plan described several community development projects that were also included in the budget. They included the development of recreation facilities and a requirement for using the Smithers Alpine Theme on all new commercial construction and remodelling projects in the downtown area.

Since the municipal and provincial governments own most of the undeveloped land within the municipality, the town has been able to make sure that the rate and location of residential developments are in keeping with the community plan. This makes the process of providing services more efficient. Development proceeds according to the population forecast and estimates of housing demand. Since 1987, Smithers has grown at a manageable rate of one percent a year. The municipality has developed enough residential lots to meet the demand for new housing in the community.

One of the most controversial issues that emerged in the planning process was the use of an abandoned forestry office site within the town which has many old-growth trees. The town's Recreation Committee preferred to see the site developed as a passive community park, and the Planning Committee wanted to develop part of the site for residential lots. This issue, along with other key planning issues, were presented to the public for input. An important part of this input came from the results of a questionnaire which was distributed to the residents of the community.

The outcome of the questionnaire indicated that residents preferred to maintain and improve their quality of life. Sixty-four percent preferred to use the forestry site as a passive family-oriented park, 93 percent supported the Smithers Alpine Theme, and 63 percent preferred moderate economic growth based upon a diversified economy, sustainable use of natural resources, and integration of environmental and social concerns.

The Smithers Official Community Plan contained a number of environmental policies. These included encouraging agricultural and recreational uses of flood-susceptible lands and avoiding residential development in these areas. The plan also discouraged building, grading, and tree harvesting on slopes that exceed 30 percent and limited development on hillsides of 20 to 30 percent to less than ten percent lot coverage.

The plan required tree planting on both sides of streets in new residential subdivisions, encouraged tree planting on slopes greater than 20 percent, and encouraged local sawmills to upgrade their waste burners to the current state-of-the-art pollution control technology. It supported recycling of glass, aluminum, paper and other materials which can be reused economically and discouraged the use of

Grant Copeland

Smithers' alpine theme.

nonbiodegradable plastic packaging materials when adequate substitutes are available. It also discouraged residential development within the 35-decibel noise cone area of the Smithers airport. These environmental policies did not completely satisfy environmental advocates in the community, but a strong majority of residents supported them.

The Smithers Council put a high priority on completing a new four-diamond ball park, developing a multipurpose perimeter trail, constructing additional tennis courts, revitalizing Central Park, landscaping the highway right-of-way, and developing nature interpretation facilities in Riverside Park. Most of these projects were completed during the ten years after the Official Community Plan was adopted.

Smithers is a model for economic diversification at the community level, and this diversification has been an important factor in protecting the surrounding environment. Unlike many other northern communities in BC, Smithers is not heavily dependent on a single industry. As a result, the community has developed an outstanding array of recreational and other amenities that, along with the local commitment to preserving visual and ecological values, contribute to a vibrant and high quality of life.

Chapter 8

NELSON: A TOWN IN TRANSITION

Grant Copeland

*Heritage revitalization of Nelson's downtown core
was instrumental in the town's economic recovery.*

Since the mid-1980s, the town of Nelson in southeastern British Columbia has changed from an economically depressed community that was heavily dependent on logging and wood products manufacturing into a more diversified and prosperous community. In 1994, a comprehensive study examined the factors that contributed to its recovery (Copeland 1994).

Between 1982 and 1992, Nelson lost 490 sawmill jobs, 260 plywood plant jobs, 100 university jobs, 450 provincial government jobs, 100 BC Telephone jobs, and 100+ Canadian Pacific Railway jobs. The combined effect of these losses was devastating to the local economy. Within a period of five years, 1981 to 1985, Nelson lost nearly a third of its work force. By 1984, the apartment vacancy rate had soared to 32 percent (compared to neighboring towns at 12 to 13 percent). Building permits fell from a ten-year average of $5.3 million to only $1.3 million in 1985. The official unemployment rate exceeded 20 percent, but because many workers took early retirement or lower paying jobs, actual joblessness and under-

Bed and breakfast facility: "Inn the Garden," is representative of many new small businesses in Nelson.

employment were probably much worse. As a result, the town's population decreased by approximately 1,000 (about 11 percent) between 1981 and 1986, and several schools closed. The real estate market was flat between 1983 and 1985, with over 500 homes listed at extremely low prices. The Salvation Army opened a soup kitchen, the first since the great depression.

By 1991-92, direct employment in the forestry sector had fallen from about 12 percent of total employment in 1981 to less than six percent. Although resource extraction will remain important to the local economy, it is unlikely that this sector will be a significant source of growth in the future. What has happened to employment in the forest industry is similar in some ways to what happened to mining employment after 1914 when Nelson's smelter shut down. Although a significant proportion of total employment disappeared, the town survived.

The key question here is how Nelson has recovered from these bleak prospects. The answer is complex because the recovery was the result of many diverse efforts that originated within the community. To a large extent, the mostly unplanned recovery was based on the community's refusal to give up hope and the unwillingness of many unemployed residents to leave their community:

The process of recovery involved a $1.2 million heritage revitalization of the town's main street. This program created 180 person years of employment in revitalization activities plus 42 new jobs in small businesses related to heritage revitalization. It also increased property values by about $2.9 million. The program restored many of Nelson's historic brick and stone buildings to their original con-

dition. The provincial government was the main source of funding for the program, with participation from the local municipal council and local businesses.

The filming locally of two major feature films, *Roxanne* and *Housekeeping*, generated a significant amount of employment and increased the sense of pride in the
community. Although companies based outside the community produced these
films, they nevertheless contributed substantially to the community's economic
recovery.

In 1988 the opening of the Canadian International College created 75 new jobs,
brought 275 Japanese students into the community, and created a significant
amount of new trade for local businesses. Although the college closed after the
1996-97 school year, other educational institutions are using Nelson's college
campus more often. Both long-time residents and newcomers have developed
small, mostly service-oriented businesses that have expanded rapidly. One estimate indicates that about 400 home-based businesses operated within a ten-
minute drive of the town in 1992 (Lacroix 1992). Women have been increasingly
active in this small business sector. The underground economy was a positive factor, too. It includes exchanging services without payment of money, mushroom
picking, and a growing amount of community volunteer activities. This period
also saw an expansion of Nelson's tourism industry, particularly guided ecotourism and the number of bed-and-breakfast establishments, which increased
about 70 percent between 1989 and 1994.

A significant number of people who have sold their homes in inflated metropolitan real estate markets have moved to Nelson where housing costs have been
considerably less and the quality of life remains relatively high. The new Nelson is
not only more diversified, it is more flexible and far more resilient to boom and
bust cycles.

Nelson's future economic vitality is closely tied to maintaining the high-quality
living environment that both residents and visitors prize. The West Kootenay
region is blessed with numerous scenic navigable lakes, some with good sports fishing; lush, accessible old-growth forests; and world-class alpine hiking, mountain
climbing, and skiing. Nelson is known as a friendly community and a relatively safe
and desirable place to raise a family or retire. Educational and health services are
excellent. Crime rates are relatively low. The town is also known for its exceptional
heritage buildings and as a place where artisans choose to live and work. The community is large enough to provide all the essential and high-demand services, but
small enough so that people find it relatively easy to know each other.

The loss of the sawmill eliminated the teepee burner and brought about a major
improvement in air quality. Another big step in protecting quality of life in and
around Nelson was the protection in 1996 of the Nelson watershed and the adjacent Lasca Creek area. The new West Arm Provincial Park extends east from
Nelson about eight kilometers towards Kootenay Lake. But the clearcutting of the
forests surrounding Nelson remains a big concern to Nelson residents.

The Whitewater Ski Resort south of Nelson contributed an estimated $3.5 mil-

Whitewater Ski Area outside Nelson.

lion to the Nelson economy during the 1992-93 season. About 40 percent of skiers were from out-of-town, mainly from Washington, Alberta, and the Vancouver area. On average, each visitor spends about $125 per day, $25 at the ski area and the remaining $100 in Nelson (Whitewater Ski Resort, 1994). This is particularly important for Nelson's tourist accommodations, which would experience lower occupancy rates during the winter without skiers visiting from Spokane, Washington, and other places outside the area. Whitewater has become well known for its exceptional snow conditions and challenging terrain.

Although unemployment rates in the Nelson area remain unacceptably high at around 12 percent, the economic future looks relatively bright there compared with many other single-industry towns in the Kootenays and elsewhere in the province. The contrast with other communities will be even more evident as employment in the forest industry shrinks to a sustainable level. Some communities will probably continue to do all they can to milk the last years of an era of unsustainable resource exploitation. But the resources will eventually run out, and these communities will face, like Nelson did, the need to diversify and build a much different economy. The degree of protection of the natural landscape and the general quality of life in and around communities will make a significant difference in how many people these communities will be able to attract following further declines in the forest industry.

If it remains a desirable environment in which to live, the Nelson area can keep its existing residents and also attract people from far and wide. This will ensure the continuation of a strong and diversified economy. There will likely be a further increase in the number of small businesses and entrepreneurs choosing to locate in Nelson. Building on the success of Selkirk College's new art and crafts facilities in Nelson, the city can eventually restore its former function as a center of education. Recently more film productions have visited in the Nelson area. Nelson's growth will accelerate as the quality of life in larger cities diminishes and the comparative mismanagement of areas elsewhere continues.

Despite these positive prospects, there is a warning inherent in growth predictions. Growth has its costs and can result, if not properly managed, in severe deterioration of the quality of life. A survey conducted by the Harmony Foundation in 1993 (Johnson Group 1993) revealed that Nelson residents are concerned about quality of life and want to see controls on the growth of their community. Although they support an appropriate amount of tourism, most residents don't want Nelson to turn into a Banff or Aspen and be overrun with tourists. Most of those interviewed felt that "a degree-granting educational facility would be a desirable way of expanding the economy without compromising the environment." They also expressed support for more small-scale and home-based businesses, secondary manufacturing, and local production of edible products.

Nelson's Official Community Plan reflects some of these concerns. The plan clearly indicates a shift away from a heavy industrial base. The waterfront, traditionally used by heavy industry, is allocated for a mix of tourist accommodations, residential, light industrial, and open spaces. A new 100-room waterfront hotel opened for business in 1996, and the municipality started developing a linear park and hiking-biking trail along the waterfront shortly after. The official plan encourages the development of home-based businesses and establishes the goal of protecting the natural setting and Nelson's "small town" character. The town council plans to keep residential densities low and the downtown "pedestrian-oriented" and to encourage a friendly "small-scale" feel. The plan emphasizes the protection of Nelson's heritage values and continues the theme of revitalizing the historic downtown area. The plan recognizes that the local cultural and arts community "adds a critical dimension to the livability of the City."

Although it contained many promising policies, the 1993 Official Community Plan also contained erroneous data and conclusions about economic trends. It also lacked sufficient substance to guide the city's economic development. These weaknesses indicate that careful planning is not responsible for Nelson's economic transition. For example, Section 2.1 of the plan claims that the service sector declined between 1981 and 1986, but Statistics Canada figures show that it actually remained nearly constant (1,460 to 1,455). The plan also wrongly states that employment in primary industries doubled between 1981 and 1986; in fact, it actually declined slightly from 210 to 205. And the plan claims that more jobs were created in government and education, when they actually experienced a slight decline from 320 to 315. This misleading information masks the real factors behind Nelson's recent economic recovery.

Also inaccurate and misleading are the forest industry's exaggerated claims regarding the effect of timber extraction and milling on other sectors of the economy. Using the forest industry's multiplier of three indirect jobs for each direct job, the loss of 310 direct jobs in the forest industry would have reduced the total number of jobs by upwards of 1,200. At 1.75 jobs per family, this would have translated to the loss of over 680 families. At 2.4 persons per family, this would have meant that the loss in forest industry employment reduced the population of Nelson by about 1,630 persons. But this did not happen. Census statistics show that the population of Nelson decreased by only 1,013 between 1981 and 1986. Many of these people left the community because of job reductions in other sectors of the economy, including the shutdown of David Thompson University (100 jobs), reduction in provincial government employment (650 jobs), and layoffs at BC Telephone (100 jobs). Although people who lived outside Nelson held many of these jobs, the figures show that many other people who lost their jobs actually stayed in Nelson. If the 380 unemployed Nelson forestry workers had decided where to live based on where they worked, they would have moved from the community to look for employment in the forest industry elsewhere. The real figures indicate that the industry's 3:1 multiplier is exaggerated and the true multiplier is actually much lower. In Nelson every two direct jobs probably produce less than one indirect job, for a multiplier of 1.5:1.

Despite the lack of comprehensive economic planning, the transition in Nelson's economy has provided a new expanded base of economic development that balances growth with a high quality of life. More accurate economic data, analysis, and planning could result in even greater enhancement of economic diversification and environmental management.

Nelson's success in restructuring its economy may hold some general lessons for us. For example, programs such as Nelson's main street revitalization project provided excellent results for funds spent and could be continued in Nelson and emulated in other communities. BC's transition to something other than an economy based on resource extraction is inevitable, and this process could benefit from a comprehensive study of the role of government economic subsidies and economic development policies and programs.

Other municipalities have recovered rapidly after downturns in their primary resource industries. In 1987 Dubois, Wyoming, lost its major employer, a sawmill. Thirty percent of the town's employment was associated with the mill. Although people feared that the local economy would never recover, the stores did not close, the people did not leave, and surprisingly, the town started to grow. For the first three years after the mill closed, real income in Dubois grew by 8.5 percent a year, much faster than the national average. Like many towns in the Greater Yellowstone area, most of Dubois' success in recovering and growing can be attributed to the fact that Dubois is a nice place to live. A survey of migrants to the town revealed that 71 percent of them moved to town for "noneconomic" reasons. Their most important considerations were the "physical setting and community tone plus residents' lifestyle and attitude" (Rasker 1994).

After the wafer board plant closed its doors in 1991 and the air quality improved, the economic situation in Kremmling, Colorado quickly responded. Housing occupancy and tax revenues increased. The community adopted an economic development strategy based on diversity and protection of its small-town friendliness and environmental quality (Rasker 1994).

There are many other communities in the western US and Canada that have prospered primarily because they offer a relatively high quality of life. Like Nelson, the natural environment of Dubois and Kremmling rate very high, and these towns have attracted (and retained) retirees and "footloose" businesses.

Chapter 9

BC's Endangered Wilderness Project: An Ongoing Struggle

Grant Copeland

Tatshenshini-Alsek River system, part of the largest protected area in the world.

Shortly before work began on the first system plan for British Columbia's provincial parks in 1987, the United Nations issued an urgent message that unlimited industrial growth demanded by the growing human population was leading to global environmental catastrophe. Resources needed for the basic survival of everyone on earth were degrading or disappearing faster than nature could restore them. The UN's World Commission on Environment and Development recommended tripling the world's protected areas from approximately four to 12 percent of the global land area (World Commission on Environment and Development 1987). Since conditions in many countries of the world preclude most preservation options, countries like Canada, Australia, and the State of Alaska in the United States, which have relatively large expanses of remaining de facto wilderness, need to set aside more than 12 percent.

In 1987, many of the negative effects cited by the UN study were apparent in BC. Crown land surrounding many communities had been extensively clearcut logged. In some cases logging had caused severe damage to domestic water supplies, and highways were washed out. In other areas, logging damage to riparian fish habitats, pulp mill pollution, and overfishing had combined to force reductions in fishing.

By 1987, the overall prospect of this damage had become a great concern to many people living in the province. Provincial environmental groups had been working hard for years to protect specific areas like the Valhalla Provincial Park in the Slocan Valley, South Moresby National Park Reserve on the Queen Charlotte Islands, the Stein Tribal Park near Vancouver, and a few others. Environmental groups across the province were putting other protected area proposals together to present to the provincial government. After spending eight years fighting for the Valhalla Park, which was finally created in 1983, the directors of the Valhalla Society in New Denver and other leading environmental activists realized that there was no hope for most of the remaining wilderness areas if government continued to consider them at the rate of only one proposal every few years.

In 1988, the BC government had no plan to meet the UN target of protecting 12 percent of the total land base. The government did not even develop the first protected area plan in BC; a nongovernment environmental organization, the Valhalla Society produced it. For years, despite requests from many environmental groups and individuals, BC Parks had steadfastly refused to prepare a comprehensive park system plan. At that time, BC parks usually resisted proposals for single parks. In response to this lack of policy, the Valhalla Society combined a number of grassroots protected area proposals into a single comprehensive plan to expand the park system from 5.2 percent to 13 percent of the provincial land area.

Community groups, local and provincial environmental organizations, and many First Nations submitted grassroots protected area proposals to the society. Weighing and comparing protected area proposals was a challenge. Some were extremely modest, and in many cases they were too small. Others simply included entire land areas traditionally used by communities or First Nations. In some regions of the province, there were many proposals; in other regions, there were no submissions, or too few. Filling out the provincial system plan required extensive work that involved meeting with people across the province and researching the knowledge of scientists and lay persons who were familiar with their regions. In the end, some of the proposed protected areas had to be reduced in size to keep the plan reasonably close to the UN target figure of 12 percent.

In 1988, the Valhalla Society printed thousands of full-color copies of the first edition of BC's Endangered Wilderness Map and distributed it widely throughout BC and Canada. However, the provincial government in Victoria rejected the first map and insulted the society's efforts. Instead of accepting the proposal for consideration, some Members of the Legislative Assembly focused on discrediting the presenters as radical environmentalists.

Three years later in 1991, BC's protected areas still comprised only 5.67 percent of the provincial land area. Fourteen of the 103 park proposals included on the

Several thousand people hiked into the headwaters of the Stein River Valley in support of the proposal to preserve the watershed as a tribal heritage park

first map had been partially logged. The boundaries of many of the protected areas proposed in 1988 needed adjusting to exclude new clearcut areas that had reduced substantially the remaining amount of pristine wilderness. At that time, one-third of the 122 areas proposed for protection on the Endangered Wilderness Map had already been logged or were scheduled for logging development within the following three years. In addition, mineral exploration or development was active in at least five areas, and three were threatened by major hydroelectric dams and transmission lines.

Meanwhile, largely in response to widespread public support for the proposed park system plan, the BC government initiated what it called Parks 90. However, most of the areas defined by Parks 90 were too small to protect wilderness and wildlife. In addition, the wilderness designation the Ministry of Forests offered did not provide full protection from resource extraction. Most of the wilderness areas the ministry identified consisted of mainly rock and ice with little or no forest values. Meanwhile, the BC public had become more aware of the negative impacts of industrial forestry on human health and quality of life, and public demand for preservation had grown.

In light of these developments, the Valhalla Society revised and updated its Endangered Wilderness Map in 1991 by analyzing new data received from the growing number of individuals and groups working on wilderness and parks issues. The revised or second version of the map incorporated improved protection of biological diversity by including areas within bioregions that were not represented previously and linking together and adding to some of the existing larger areas. The primary focus was on proposed areas that exceeded 1,000 hectares. The second map included linear corridors, heritage rivers, and trails as areas that warranted protection. Many of the areas proposed for protection are subject to the eventual settlement of aboriginal land claims.

Following the publication of the first version of the map, a large, year-long project by Simon Fraser University (SFU) graduate students assessed the proposal's impact on the forest industry (Natural Resources Management Program – SFU 1990). They calculated that creating all 103 proposed new parks would reduce the Allowable Annual Cut by 3.5 percent. The Valhalla Society had estimated three percent, and the forest industry had initially claimed the loss would be 15 percent. A month after the release of the SFU report, a prominent spokesperson for the forest industry stated that the industry had done its own study and arrived at the same figures as SFU. Since then, however, it has come to light that at least one major forest company exaggerated the timber volume figures reported to the SFU team. Instead of a loss of 3.5 percent, a more accurate estimate would probably be 2.5 to 3 percent.

The SFU team estimated that 2,554 direct jobs in the forest industry would be affected if all the proposals were enacted at once and if there were no offsetting policies in place. However, the team pointed to a study which showed that a single investment of $600 million in value-added manufacturing could create 3,900 jobs. The SFU study stated that without any new investment, improved sawmill efficiency could produce 30 percent more wood than the amount removed from the Allowable Annual Cut by the 1988 proposals. Improved forest practices could create even more forest industry jobs.

The second edition of BC's Endangered Wilderness map included an inset map of commercially viable forests in the province. These forests do not include alpine, subalpine, grassland, or noncommercial areas. The Ministry of Forests defines noncommercial areas as "blocks over 5,000 hectares not accessible from the provincial highway system by better than a seasonal four-wheel-drive standard road and with no plans to develop for access within 20 years." The inset map shows a small proportion of commercially viable forest within the proposed parks system. In dramatic comparison, a vast area remains available to industry. The large areas which are not commercially viable include alpine areas and the northern boreal forests and plateaus. This inset map helped counter the phobias and resistance of the forest industry, which was falsely claiming that saving the proposed protected areas would have a large impact on logging in the province.

When the second version of BC's Endangered Wilderness Map appeared in 1991, the forest industry employed only 0.93 workers in BC per 1,000 cubic meters of wood cut, compared to an average of 1.5 across Canada. If BC had even met the national average of 1.5 jobs per 1,000 cubic meters, the industry could have provided almost 50,000 more forest industry jobs in 1988. Better yet, it could have maintained the existing number of jobs by cutting far less wood, and this would

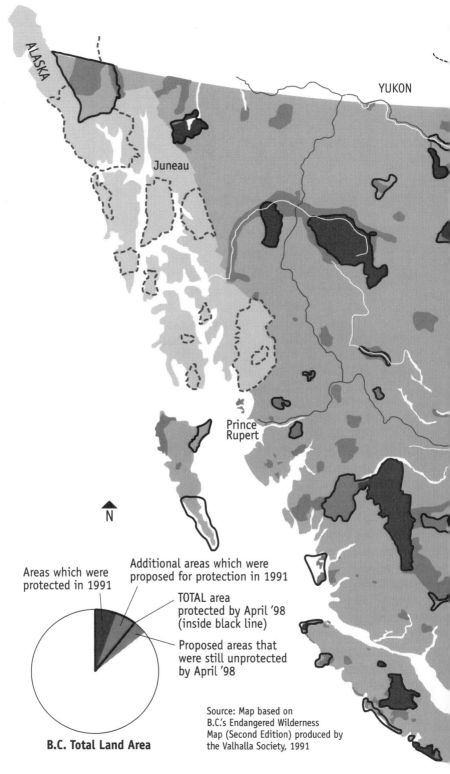

ALASKA

YUKON

Juneau

Prince
Rupert

N

Areas which were
protected in 1991

Additional areas which were
proposed for protection in 1991

TOTAL area
protected by April '98
(inside black line)

Proposed areas that
were still unprotected
by April '98

B.C. Total Land Area

Source: Map based on
B.C.'s Endangered Wilderness
Map (Second Edition) produced by
the Valhalla Society, 1991

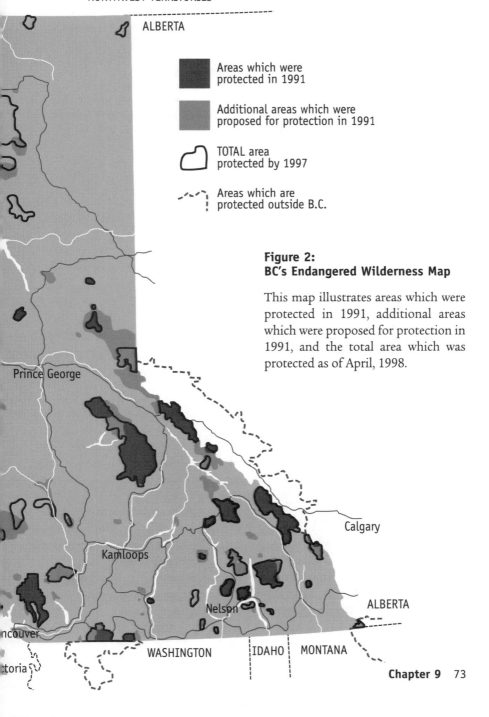

NORTHWEST TERRITORIES

ALBERTA

Areas which were
protected in 1991

Additional areas which were
proposed for protection in 1991

TOTAL area
protected by 1997

Areas which are
protected outside B.C.

Figure 2:
BC's Endangered Wilderness Map

This map illustrates areas which were
protected in 1991, additional areas
which were proposed for protection in
1991, and the total area which was
protected as of April, 1998.

Prince George

Calgary

Kamloops

Nelson

ALBERTA

ncouver

:toria

WASHINGTON   IDAHO   MONTANA

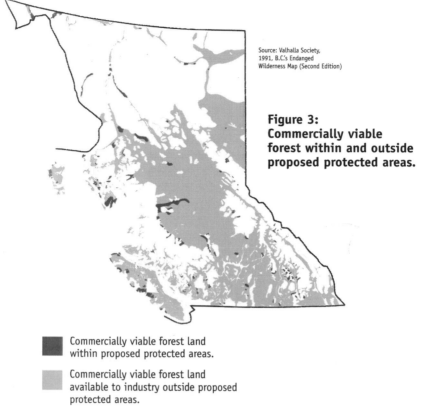

Source: Valhalla Society, 1991, B.C.'s Endanged Wilderness Map (Second Edition)

**Figure 3:
Commercially viable
forest within and outside
proposed protected areas.**

■ Commercially viable forest land
within proposed protected areas.

░ Commercially viable forest land
available to industry outside proposed
protected areas.

Commercially viable forest does not include alpine, sub-alpine, grassland or non-commercial areas defined by the Ministry of Forests as "blocks over 5,000 ha not accessible from provincial highway system by better than a seasonal 4WD standard road and with no plans to develop for access within 20 years."

have made our forests last longer.

"Diversity is the key to balance in natural systems: diverse species, diverse genetic pools, diverse age groups, and diverse landscapes. Protected areas must be large enough to preserve this diversity. The disappearance of one species leads to others, for they are all dependent upon one another in this fragile "web of life." Human survival is also dependent upon this web, which has, as its foundation, the millions of microscopic species which feed the fish and nourish the forests and food crops. Biodiversity requirements were the reason for expanding the size of several protected areas on the second version of the map" (Valhalla Society 1991).

The second edition of the wilderness map included at least one proposal from each of 63 of BC's 73 distinct bioregions. The remaining ten bioregions either do not contain significant wilderness, or they require more analysis.

The second version of the map recommended protecting 14.14 percent (13,413,147 hectares, 134,131 square kilometers, 33,278,742 acres, or 51,998

Alsek Lake, part of the largest wilderness area in the world.

square miles) of BC's land base. If protected, these areas would include more land than the three Canadian provinces of New Brunswick, Nova Scotia, and Prince Edward Island combined, or 76 percent of Washington State. Though vast in size, these existing and proposed protected areas contain less than six percent of the commercially viable timber in British Columbia. Protected areas include national parks and marine parks, national wildlife sanctuaries, provincial Class A and marine parks, roadless wilderness areas, wilderness conservancies, ecological reserves, and tribal parks.

In 1993, the BC government revealed its Protected Areas Strategy, which established the policies and procedures needed to double the amount of protected areas in British Columbia from six to 12 percent by the year 2000. About the same time, the Canadian Parliament adopted the goal of protecting 12 percent of Canada.

In conjunction with the provincial Protected Areas Strategy, the BC government began the process of developing land-use plans (regional plans and subregional Land and Resource Management Plans) that included recommendations on protected areas. In 1991, 52 ecosystem types had little or no representation in protected areas. As of 1998, only 17 are not represented. As of April 1998 the total protected area in British Columbia had increased to over ten million hectares, or 10.6 percent of the province. Between 1991 and January 1998, more than 285 new protected area and/or park additions totaling more than four million hectares, were established in BC. Many of these newly protected areas conform closely with areas recommended on the Valhalla Society's Endangered Wilderness Map.

Over 80 percent of the province has been or is currently being planned under comprehensive land-use plans. Regional land-use plans are in place for the Vancouver Island, Cariboo-Chilcotin, and Kootenay-Boundary regions, while sub-regional Land and Resource Management Plans (LRMP) are in place or are being developed in 18 subregions of the province.

A variety of globally significant ecologically representative areas and features are now protected in British Columbia. These include parts of the northern Rocky Mountain region known as the Muskwa-Kechika, one of North America's last true wilderness areas south of the 60th parallel; the Kitlope watershed on the midcoast, the largest remaining pristine temperate rainforest watershed in the world; the internationally significant South Moresby National Park and National Marine Park on the Queen Charlotte Islands; the Stein Valley, one of the last remaining untouched watersheds in southwestern BC; and the Tatshenshini, which connects with other protected areas in Alaska and the Yukon to form the largest protected area on earth.

The Endangered Wilderness Map project offers several important lessons. First, problems as complex as this need a systems approach. Piecemeal efforts are insufficient because they address only a small part of the larger landscape of ecosystems or geographical area.

Second, government will not take bold action without a big push from an interested public. In this case, the initiative for change came from the collective efforts of a multitude of nongovernment environmental organizations from across BC who allowed their proposals to form part of a broad-based system plan. Although there are many capable people working for government, the nature of the political-governmental system inhibits innovation. Some key government workers made valuable contributions to the development and refinement of the system plan, but they usually delivered their information in unmarked parcels or by other clandestine means of communication.

A third lesson is that nongovernment activists need to provide leadership. Someone has to coordinate, to take the ball and run with it and follow through and finish the mission. In this case the Valhalla Society took on this responsibility. In other campaigns, other groups have led the struggle for change: for example, Greenpeace's interventions on the high seas or its European boycotts, the Western Canada Wilderness Committee's leadership in broadly educating the public on environmental issues, and the Sierra Club's lead role on Vancouver Island in the development of state-of-the-art GIS mapping and resource economics.

The endangered wilderness mapping project is an important case study because the changes it has influenced in BC and, by example, in other parts of the world will have lasting value for future generations. The work on this project continues in the form of campaigns to preserve more of the Stikine, the largely unprotected midcoast area, and other areas that remain inadequately protected.

Chapter 10

STIKINE WATERSHED PLANNING: UNFINISHED BUSINESS

Grant Copeland

Spatsizi River, a tributary of the Stikine,
with Red Goat Mountain in the background; part of BC's Serengeti.

The Stikine River, with its 640-kilometer (400-mile) long main stem and tributaries, is one of the last free-flowing, navigable wilderness rivers in North America. The Stikine is an international river that passes through two countries. The river flows from its headwaters in British Columbia's expansive and serenely beautiful Spatsizi Wilderness Park, though Canada's awesome Grand Canyon of the Stikine, past the tiny, charming riverside community of Telegraph Creek, BC, and finally cuts through the great coast mountains and glaciers on its way to meet the sea in southeast Alaska. The coastal Tlingit people, who for many centuries shared the lower Stikine with the Tahltans, simply called it "The Great River."

Because of the Stikine watershed's remote location and size, many diverse wildlife populations have survived in and roam freely through the huge 20,000-square-mile area. There are few comparable areas left in the world where such a

Mountain Goats in the Grand Canyon of the Stikine.

great variety of wildlife still coexists in natural balance, complete with prey and predator relationships.

Wolves, grizzly and black bears, mountain goats, stone sheep, caribou, moose, bald eagles and gyrfalcons are examples of the abundant wildlife living in the vastness of the Stikine's mountain ranges, expansive alpine tundra, and river valleys. This wilderness setting offers opportunities for a great many forms of recreation, such as hunting, camping, hiking, wildlife photography, cross-country skiing, canoeing, kayaking, river rafting, and others. Rainbow trout, Arctic grayling, Dolly Varden, salmon, and other species are abundant in the numerous rivers, creeks, and lakes. The Stikine accommodates the Spatsizi herd of about 1,800 Osborne caribou, the largest known herd in BC. The Grand Canyon of the Stikine, with 300 resident mountain goats, is truly inspiring. Along the lower Stikine, grizzlies are sometimes visible feeding on salmon in a coastal rain forest setting. The numbers and diversity of wildlife in the Stikine are of global significance because there are few places south of the 60th parallel that can provide habitat of a similar quality. For these reasons, the Stikine has long been known as British Columbia's Serengeti.

At present, the Stikine River's unique character remains intact. The United States government approved wilderness status in December of 1980 for the part of the lower Stikine that flows through southeast Alaska. This US Stikine-LeConte wilderness area is managed primarily for recreation, including cabins and a remote hot spring development. But without adequate protection of the Canadian portion of the Great River, the pristine character of the Stikine could be lost forever.

Planning for land use, protected areas, and economic development in the Stikine River watershed is a complex and challenging project. I first became involved with the Stikine when BC Hydro was attempting to develop its proposed multibillion-dollar, 2,900 megawatt hydroelectric generation and transmission project during the late 1970s. Construction of this five-dam system would flood most of the Stikine's Grand Canyon and part of the upper river and transform the area into a fluctuating reservoir, blocking wildlife movements, altering the flow of the excellent salmon habitat below the Grand Canyon, and damaging much of the unique and spectacular natural scenery. The Tahltan Tribal Association hired me as part of a team to evaluate the effects of the proposed project.

The profound social and environmental effects of large dams has been well documented. According to one study (Goldsmith 1984), the job creation potential of large dams, even during the construction phase, has historically been overestimated. After construction, large dams provide few jobs. There has been a tendency to overestimate the life of dams, underestimate the costs of decommissioning them, inadequately account for the cost of the land that is flooded, overestimate the benefits of recreation, and overestimate economic benefits.

As it turned out, widespread and near unanimous objection to the dams from the local community and elsewhere in the province caused BC Hydro to defer the project and, as a result, the impact assessment work was not completed. Today, although the *Fish Protection Act*: Section 4(1) states that the main stem of the Stikine is a protected river and Section 4(3) states that a bank-to-bank dam cannot be constructed anywhere on a protected river, the Cassiar-Iskut Stikine LRMP Table[2] has requested further evidence from BC Hydro to confirm that the proposed hydroelectric project is no longer in their long-term system plan.

As a result of public pressure and evidence produced by environmental groups and ratepayer organizations, BC Hydro has shifted focus from supply side management (e.g., construction of large hydroelectric projects) to demand side management (e.g., energy conservation). Environmental groups began pushing for a comprehensive study of energy conservation in BC during the late 1980s. As a result of this effort, BC Hydro launched a review in 1991 to develop comprehensive and reliable estimates of the potential for electricity conservation in BC. The findings of this study revealed that energy conservation could produce 22,000 to 27,000 gigawatt-hours of electricity at rates less than the cost of new sources of electricity supply (Collaborative Committee for the 1991-94 Conservation Potential Review 1994). To put this amount into perspective, the economic potential of conservation is greater than all of the electricity BC Hydro sold in the lower mainland of BC in 1992-93. Expressed another way, the potential is equivalent to four new dams the size of BC Hydro's Revelstoke Dam.

A multistakeholder collaborative committee conducted this study of the potential benefits from conservation. Although BC Hydro actively participated in and

---

2: A multistakeholder planning group that reports directly to the cabinet.

Rafting on the upper Stikine River.

funded the deliberations of the committee, it did not control the process or the results of the study. The committee initiated the project and set the terms of reference for the study. This project was similar to the BC Endangered Wilderness Map project in that it was initiated not by government, but by nongovernment activism.

The Stikine megaproject is much different from the recently developed three megawatt hydroelectric Huey Lakes project southwest of Dease Lake. This much smaller project will cause comparatively little environmental impact and is justifiable in terms of reducing dependence on imported fossil fuels to generate electricity for local consumption.

About the same time that BC Hydro was investigating its proposed Stikine hydroelectric project, Gulf Canada was testing for development of a 1.5 to 3.5 million tonnes per year anthracite coal mine in the fragile headwaters area of the Klappan, Nass, Skeena, and Spatsizi rivers. This open-pit mining project threatened to pollute most of the Stikine river system, as well as disrupt an important caribou calving area. Gulf mined and shipped truckloads of this coal overseas for testing. However, the low global demand for the high-quality anthracite coal declined, and the project did not proceed.

Clearcut logging of Sitka spruce stands had also started along the lower section of the river and more was in store for other areas, from the US border past Great Glacier and Mud Glacier, through the area Sierra Club founder John Muir described as "a Yosemite 100 miles long." The logging of the giant Sitka spruce

Salmon fishing in front of the Great Glacier, Lower Stikine River.

and cottonwood trees along the lower river in BC employed none of the local people and was taking place despite a strong local consensus calling for a moratorium on logging along the lower river. All of these logs were being sold, unprocessed, for export from the Alaskan port of Wrangell. However, the high costs of logging this remote area did not generate enough revenue, and the logging stopped.

These proposed megaprojects promised to create large, remote work camps and access roads, but sustainable long-term employment prospects for the Tahltan people living in the area were doubtful. Although large portions of the Stikine watershed are currently represented in the existing Spatsizi and Mt. Edziza provincial parks, most of the watershed remains vulnerable to industrial development and needs additional protection. The continuation of traditional First Nations uses of the Stikine and the growing tourism industry both depend upon preservation of the wilderness character of the Stikine.

The Stikine is located within Canada's Natural Region 7, which is unrepresented in the National Parks System. Parks Canada has identified two Natural Areas of Canadian Significance (NACS) in the Stikine: the Spatsizi Plateau and the Mt. Edziza area. These are joined by a Natural Site of Canadian Significance (NSCS), the Grand Canyon of the Stikine. No other canyon in Canada is proportionally as long, deep, and narrow or as spectacular in character. This combination of nationally recognized features is rare in Canada and the world.

A Parks Canada survey team recommended the Stikine "most highly" during the early 1970s as one of the most important rivers in Canada to be included in the

*BC environmental activists participating in the
1985 Canadian Assembly on National Parks and Protected Areas.
Top row, L to R: Thom Henley, Islands Protection Society; Colleen McCrory, Save South
Moresby Committee; Vicki Husband, Friends of Clayquot Sound; Connie Harris, Salmon Arm;
Peter Rowlands, Friends of the Stikine; Lynn Thunderstorm, Residents for a Free-Flowing
Stikine; John McCandless, Lilloet Tribal Council.
Bottom Row, L to R: Grant Copeland, Valhalla Wilderness Society;
Tom Manson, Yukon Conservation Society.*

Canadian Heritage River Program. The Stikine River is exceptional in that it provides an extended wilderness float trip for paddlers of moderate skills, from headwaters to ocean (with a portage around the canyon). In a workshop held in
Telegraph Creek, BC, during May 1985 representatives of environmental groups
from BC and Alaska proposed a 3.5 million hectare Stikine National Park Reserve
to protect the entire Canadian portion of the Stikine. The workshop participants
also resolved to support the native people in their pursuit of a just settlement of
their aboriginal land claims. If a Stikine National Park is established, it would be
subject to settlement of the Tahltan land claim.

Later during 1985, the Vancouver-based Friends of the Stikine distributed a
four-color visitor's guide and map of the Stikine national park reserve proposal
(Friends of the Stikine 1985). However, the Tahltan people opposed the national
park idea because they felt it would prejudice their land claim settlement process.
Their opposition was not surprising, considering that they had been left out of the
process of establishing and managing protected areas within their traditional territory. Nevertheless, the Stikine National Park proposal received national and
international support from the 1985 Heritage for Tomorrow Canadian Assembly

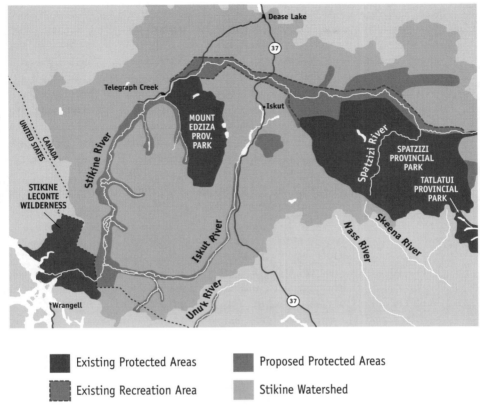

Existing Protected Areas

Proposed Protected Areas

Existing Recreation Area

Stikine Watershed

Figure 4:
Map of proposed protected areas in the Stikine watershed,
which includes parts of northern BC and southeast Alaska.

on National Parks and Protected Areas held in Banff, Alberta, and from the 1986 meeting of the World Wilderness Congress in Colorado. The existing protected areas in the Stikine were established through a gradual process. Mt. Edziza was the first park to be created in the area, but it was not designated as a Class A Park until 1972. In the absence of a master plan, the government prepared a very sketchy interim policy statement in 1976.

Spatsizi Plateau Wilderness Park, encompassing approximately 675,000 hectares, is one of the largest and most diverse parks in the province. The NDP government established it by Order-in-Council in 1975, shortly before the government was voted out of power. The first master plan for Spatsizi Park was developed in 1980. During 1987, following a recommendation from the province's Wilderness Advisory Committee, another Order-in-Council designated the 217,000-hectare Stikine River Recreation Area which links Mt. Edziza and Spatsizi parks. BC Parks prepared an interim management plan for the recreation area in

1991. Although the provincial government considers this area a protected area and includes it on the map of protected areas, the current protection is incomplete. Mining exploration and development is allowed within the recreation area, and the entire area is under discussion through the LRMP process, which will produce recommendations for the future use of the area.

The section of the Stikine River between the US border and Telegraph Creek also remains unprotected. The Ministry of Forests prepared a management plan for this area in 1989 (Lower Stikine Management Plan). This plan includes some limits on logging but does not prohibit mining or road construction. The Ministry of Forests management plan did nothing to stop considerable damage to the riverine ecology by a large hovercraft which was used to haul diesel fuel and ore in the area during the mid-1990s. The use of the hovercraft continued until the Friends of the Stikine and its president Peter Rowlands launched a lawsuit.

BC Parks prepared a brief Interim Recreation Management Statement for Mt. Edziza and Spatsizi parks and the Stikine Recreation Area in 1997. This statement is the current guide for the management of the parks. Although these areas, in combination with the adjacent Tatlatui Park, constitute the largest protected area in the province (1.2 million hectares), the interim management document is only 23 pages long. The statement does not mention the traditional Tahltan use of the area.

Although the Lower Stikine Management Plan briefly describes the issue of the Tahltan people and their traditional land use activities, none of the plans for this area have involved the active participation of the Tahltan people. Nor has the government sufficiently considered and integrated Tahltan culture into management policies. BC Parks developed all of the park plans and interim management statements in-house with little opportunity for public involvement. There have been several anecdotal reports of park authorities attempting to prohibit Tahltan activities within the protected areas. Several Tahltan people work on a seasonal basis for BC Parks, but a full-time non-Tahltan superintendent manages the two parks and the recreation area, and non-Tahltans make all of the management decisions.

The Cassiar-Iskut-Stikine LRMP table was set up in March of 1997 and has been meeting roughly once a month since then. Table members include representatives of the Tahltan Tribal Council, mining company representatives, local residents, local business owners, a few people who live in the region but outside the study area, numerous government agency representatives, and representatives of the Friends of the Stikine.

The findings of an economic study for the Stikine (Copeland and Nicol 1998) indicated that prospects for integrated economic development within the LRMP area are excellent. The term "integrated development" refers to a diversity of economic projects that produce minimum detrimental effects across the various economic sectors. These projects tend to be environmentally benign and provide optimum employment and other social benefits. They also generate jobs and revenue for local residents and provide the highest long-term economic benefits to the province and the nation.

The economic study found significant opportunities in each of the major forest-related economic sectors examined – tourism, fishing, forestry, and mining. In addition, and perhaps more important for the local communities, appropriate training will enable residents of the area to capture a greater proportion of employment benefits. The study found that tourism is the largest sector of employment for local people. Although traditional tourism focused on guide-outfitting, sustainable wildlife hunting reached its limit decades ago. Today, nonconsumptive ecotourism and back-country recreation present opportunities for additional tourism activities.

The largest employment sector is mining, but only a small percentage of the miners are local residents. Forestry activities were relatively dormant between 1997 and 1999. Most of the members of the LRMP table are opposed to large-scale clearcut logging. A number of residents are involved in the Stikine commercial fishery, but most of the Stikine salmon have been allocated to Alaska fishermen under an international agreement, and the Alaskans have been harvesting even more than their allotment.

BC's chief forester recently arbitrarily increased the Allowable Annual Cut for the 13.5-million-hectare Cassiar Timber Supply Area from 140,000 to 400,000 cubic metres, even though the industry is currently not interested in logging in this remote area. The chief forester's report lacks ecological rational and mathematical logic for the increase in the allowable cut. In place of large industrial forestry, a small community forest license or tree farm license in the range of 25,000 to 50,000 cubic meters per year makes more sense when considered within the context of overall, integrated economic development options and local preferences.

As the LRMP planning process progressed, it became obvious that the main land use conflict is between mining (particularly mining access roads) and wilderness protection for wildlife and associated wilderness-based recreation activities and tourism. Resource extraction can take place in large areas such as the Stikine without damaging the wilderness environment, but without economic and political commitments to preserve the wilderness, environmental degradation will always be a threat. It should be relatively easy to maintain a high-quality environment in the LRMP area because the natural resources there remain largely intact. Local residents place high values on their quality of life and want to maintain and protect it.

Opportunities exist for increased involvement of the Tahltan First Nation in resource management of their traditional territory, which includes the entire LRMP study area. Not only have the Tahltan people been excluded from many decision-making processes that affect the management of protected areas in their territory, they have not been consulted on a whole range of land-use issues. These include the setting of allowable annual cuts and related logging along Highway 37 at the south end of the LRMP planning area, large scale development of mining properties in many locations throughout the area, and the planning of hydroelectric megaprojects. The 1997 Delgamuukw Supreme Court of Canada decision confirmed that First Nations have a substantial legal interest in the land they have traditionally used. There is no longer any question that aboriginal people have a fundamental right to be involved in land-use decision making.

After the LRMP planning process is completed, the existing Interim Recreation Management Statement for the protected areas of the Stikine should be expanded into a more definitive management plan. There is an urgent need for research and collective planning to determine the capacity of the Stikine River and back country to accommodate and sustain appropriate levels of recreation activities and tourism. This work is necessary to achieve an acceptable balance between conservation goals and recreation/tourism use. Research on carrying capacity would also be helpful to the LRMP planning process.

The LRMP table has considered a number of scenarios, including one which would increase fully protected areas within the study area to approximately 30 percent and provide special management protection of most of the remaining parts of the area. In this scenario, most of the special management provisions would place a high value on maintaining wildlife habitat and minimize the construction of access roads.

Adding the lower Stikine River to the protected area system and expanding the BC Parks budget within the Cassiar-Iskut-Stikine LRMP area would generate significant benefits. There is an excellent opportunity to extend the work season of existing BC Parks employees as recommended by the BC Parks supervisor and achieve more active participation of the Tahltan First Nation in the future planning and management of the protected areas within the LRMP area.

This example and the other case studies in this section demonstrate the possibility of making ecological economics a part of land-use planning at the community and provincial levels. However, these projects are more like experiments than solutions. Land-use and resource management decisions are much too complex for simple or universal solutions. We need more real-world experimentation before we can claim that our management efforts are meeting the challenges of ecological economics or community-based planning. We need to move much more quickly to make changes in the way we manage our collective resources.

The five case studies in this section contain a couple of key lessons.

First, advocacy by nongovernment groups is usually essential for achieving substantial changes in the way society manages economic development or deals with pressing environmental/ecological issues. Public advocacy is especially important for integrating ecological considerations with economics. Corporations, banks, and the investment industry have traditionally controlled economic development. These institutions are primarily interested in profits and return on shareholder equity. They may be concerned with the way ecological or social concerns affect the bottom line, but they seldom make decisions based on these concerns. The key challenge before us is to counter the force of traditional economics by making more effective use of informed public input and balanced multistakeholder involvement in public decision making.

The second lesson concerns the need for more accurate and up-to-date information on ecological economics. The public and its elected representatives and public servants often feel frustrated by information gaps on basic economics as well as on ecology. Most governments today seem to be operating in an information vacuum. This may not be surprising, given the speed with which communities around the world must respond to a rapidly changing array of economic opportunities and barriers.

It sometimes seems that elected representatives do not understand today's constantly changing economic realities because they lack accurate and up-to-date information. Or perhaps pressure from special interests makes it easier and safer for them to ignore the need for change. These pressures usually favor the substantial resources that only major and well-organized industrial interests can afford to expend in the quest to maintain their positions in the world marketplace. Both explanations may play a part in this dilemma. There is a third, more worrying, possibility. Governments and planning officials may take the ostrich approach of avoiding decisions altogether because they care more about their jobs or their retirement package than about our collective future. In any case, the failure to change feeds into the growing globalization of the economy and the increasing powerlessness of communities.

The public's best option is to get more involved in working for change, especially in conducting real-world experiments. Only through taking the bull by the horns and actually wrestling with change can we achieve a more balanced application of ecological economics. This will require a greater measure of well-principled entrepreneurial and activist energy than society has been able to muster thus far, plus a greater willingness on the part of elected representatives and public servants to pay more attention to these efforts.

Acts of Balance
Part 4:

PRESERVING CULTURAL DIVERSITY: THE ULTIMATE CHALLENGE

Overview

The relationship between biological, cultural, and economic diversity is perhaps the world's most important yet most neglected subject. Every day we hear news reports about ethnic and religious warfare and about people scrambling for more control of the world's finite geography and scarce resources. Reductions in biological and cultural diversity are inexorably linked to this demand for geographic territory. Today multinational corporations are responsible for most of the quest for resources as they seek to maximize their profits in disregard of the rights of indigenous people and local communities.

Wade Davis has traveled to the most remote regions of the earth to learn how indigenous people live in their environments. He studied ethnobotany at Harvard to learn about the relationships between indigenous people and the plants they use. In the final chapter of *The Clouded Leopard* (Davis 1998), Davis eloquently describes the relationship between cultural and biological diversity.

"If there is one lesson that I have drawn from my travels, it is that cultural and biological diversity are far more than the foundation of stability, they are an article of faith, a fundamental truth that indicates the way things are supposed to be. If diversity is a source of wonder, its opposite – the ubiquitous condensation to some blandly amorphous and singularly generic modern culture that I have witnessed in all parts of the world – is a source of dismay.

"We are living in the midst of an ecological catastrophe every bit as tragic as that of the slaughter of the buffalo and the passenger pigeon. Wherever one looks, there are governmental policies that are equally blind, economic rationales equally compelling. All memory is convulsed in an upheaval of violence. There is a fire burning over the Earth, taking with it plants and animals, cultures, languages, ancient skills and visionary wisdom. Quelling this flame and reinventing the poetry of diversity is the most important challenge of our times."

One of the worst atrocities in recent history was China's takeover of Tibet. Tibet had for centuries maintained a strong independence and self-reliance. Trade with other countries was negligible. Over 60 percent of the country's population were devout Buddhists who believed in the reincarnation and authority of their spiritual leader, his Holiness, the 14th Dali Lama. When the Chinese government invaded this relatively peaceful and spiritual country, most of the world remained silent and refused to help the Tibetan people. Martin Sorcese's recent film *Kundun* graphically and artfully portrays the story of the Dali Lama and the Chinese invasion of Tibet. What happened and continues to happen in Tibet represents perhaps the worst type of tragedy – greed for power, conquest, and colonialism driving a refusal to recognize human rights and cultural diversity.

Tibet's experience is far from unique. The United Nations recently recognized

Gerry Copeland

Tibetan influenced agriculture and architecture. Mustang Province, Nepal.

Canada as the best place in the world to live, yet Canada's relationship with First Nations peoples is a shameful story. From the time Europeans first visited North America, they have shown repeated disregard and disrespect for the indigenous people who had lived on the continent for thousands of years. We have literally stolen their land, decimated the buffalo and other wildlife upon which they depended, and forcefully removed their children from their families and communities and confined them in residential schools operated by our churches. In these residential schools, children were punished for speaking their native tongue and were often sexually abused. Catholicism and Protestantism replaced or at least diluted aboriginal spirituality.

Nepali family.

In the Yukon and elsewhere in Canada, laws prohibited First Nations people from operating their own businesses. Until recently, Indian guides could work only for white guide-outfitters. They were prohibited from practicing important aspects of their culture such as sharing their wealth in potlatches. And they were not allowed to vote until the middle of the 20th century. Tragically, many First Nations communities have disintegrated under Canada's policy of assimilation. Most First Nations people were herded onto small reserves where social and economic conditions have generally remained abysmal. Worst of all, the intention of governments has been to make First Nations people behave like Europeans.

Non-native people can take lessons from the traditional ways of living in harmony with nature that First Nations people practiced. The traditional life style of aboriginal people persisted for thousands of years because they lived close to the land and had great respect and appreciation for the resources from which they drew their sustenance. Their ability and willingness to share what they have with each other is another admirable quality.

An excellent model for this learning has been developed in Rediscovery Camps (Thom Henley 1989) such as those in the Stein River Valley, in the Kitlope, and on the Queen Charlotte Islands. Rediscovery Camps provide opportunities for youth of diverse cultures to learn about themselves and the rest of nature. For some First Nations, rediscovery camps have been an important catalyst for regaining and developing their traditional arts and crafts and restoring and maintaining their cultural continuity. In the words of David Suzuki "I cannot conceive of a more important program than Rediscovery. Everyone in North America, old and young, should have the chance to take part."

Although we cannot fall back to living the traditional life style of aboriginal people, we must learn how to live on our planet in a more sustainable way. We must learn how to resolve the ongoing tragedy in our relationship with other life on the planet. Unless we learn to integrate what Albert Schweitzer called "reverence for life" into the way we live our lives, we will persist in the destructive, intrusive exploitation and wanton disregard for environmental and social context that has imperiled humanity, the earth, and its atmosphere and that has already driven many species and human cultures into extinction. Amidst this despoliation, we need a new nondestructive human being who takes on the color of the terrain and atmosphere, taking only what is necessary to survive and share with others.

Governments in the United States and Canada have slowly started to recognize the wrongful ways they have treated First Nations people. In its landmark December 1997 *Delgamuukw* decision, the Supreme Court of Canada ruled that First Nations must be consulted regarding resource development within their traditional territories and that their oral history of land title is equally as important as written records of land title in defining their legitimate territories. Canada's highest court has ruled that land-use activities on aboriginal title lands cannot destroy the bond between aboriginal people and the land.

Many First Nations are working hard to adapt to the fast-changing economies of the world while also struggling to maintain cultural continuity. Every day the residents of the remote arctic community of Old Crow watch satellite television broadcasts from Atlanta, Chicago, and Los Angeles. They crave the material objects advertised on TV. They play basketball and hockey and are familiar with NBA and NHL stars. More and more, the main difference between them and non-aboriginals is their desire to preserve their traditional way of life and their close ties to their land.

The Old Crow people still depend on hunting the caribou that migrate through the immense landscape that surrounds their community. When I visited the village of Old Crow (located above the arctic circle in Yukon Territory) in the early summer of 1986, their school and band offices were heated by diesel fuel flown by

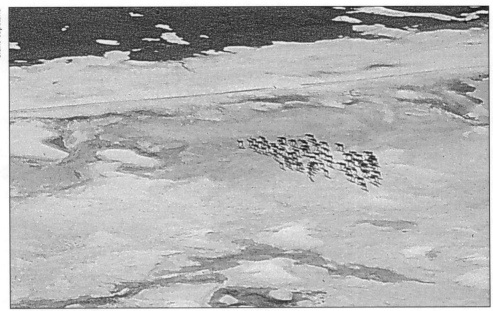

Caribou on Old Crow River.

Hercules aircraft to the airport adjacent to their community at a cost of at $6 to $8 per gallon. Snowmobiles and four-wheelers were everywhere in the village. I went out with some of their hunters after midnight to hunt caribou. The next day I was offered some of this delicious meat for lunch and visited with a group of elderly women who gathered together to sing and tell stories while they mended children's clothing. The spirit of the Old Crow people was still strong. They were concerned about protecting Old Crow flats where they trap muskrat, and they opposed oil drilling on the north slope of Alaska because they didn't want the calving grounds of the Porcupine caribou herd disrupted. Despite conflicts between their traditional lifestyle and their use of modern technology, they are committed to maintaining their hunting culture and their strong sense of family and community.

The two case studies in this section draw on over 20 years experience working with First Nations in northern BC and Yukon as an economic and environmental planning consultant. Looking back on this work, I feel privileged to have been exposed to their fascinating and diverse cultures and to have participated in their efforts to protect traditional territories and generate economic development that is relatively benign environmentally and appropriate to their traditional life styles. This work has included general land-use planning, advocating and supporting wilderness protection, planning for the joint management of parks, drafting economic development strategies, tourism development planning, and participating as an advisor to the Nisga'a in Canada's most comprehensive land claim settlement.

My experience working with First Nations people has shown me that cultural diversity is closely related to ecological diversity. First Nation cultures adapted their ways of life to the limits of the ecology where they lived. This was necessary because they lived off the land and their communities had to be self-sufficient. In many cases adaptation was essential for their survival. Understanding the necessity of adapting our cultures to the need to maintain ecological diversity can guide us in efforts to develop appropriate economic enterprises. I am convinced that cultural continuity and ecological integrity are essential prerequisites to the science and art of practicing ecological economics.

Chapter 11 focuses on the Nisga'a nation, which has been immersed in the resolution of its outstanding land claim and has maintained an exceptionally strong sense of community. Chapter 12 describes the successful campaign of the Haisla nation to protect the Kitlope, the largest remaining pristine temperate rain forest in the world.

Nisga'a Land Settlement: Delayed Justice

Nisga's pole raising.

The Nisga'a treaty is the first Canadian treaty to establish First Nations self-government and jurisdiction over the land. The Nisga'a treaty will be entrenched in the Canadian Constitution. In accepting the agreement, the Nisga'a have given up rights to most of their traditional territory. The Nisga'a Land which the treaty deeds to the Nisga'a nation is only a fraction of their traditional territory. It amounts to 1,992 square kilometers, including the lower part of the Nass River watershed and the four existing Nisga'a villages that are located along this section of the river. Non-Nisga'a logging companies have clearcut much of Nisga'a Land, which consequently needs substantial silvicultural work.

The treaty also gives the Nisga'a nation fee simple title to two categories of land outside the borders of Nisga'a Land. This land includes approximately 25 square kilometers at 18 sites which are currently reserves and 2.5 square kilometers at 15 additional new sites selected by the Nisga'a from within their traditional territory located outside Nisga'a Land. These smaller parcels of land were selected primarily for use in the development of future ecotourism and other Nisga'a economic development activities.

The Nisga'a nation will have control over forest resources on Nisga'a Land subject to provisions for a smooth transition from present logging activities. However, decades of overcutting and mismanagement have abused the forests in the Nass River region. By the government's own estimate, the rate of logging in this area has been roughly three times the sustainable rate in recent years. These conditions effectively preclude the Nisga'a from making a quick transition from the volume-based industrial logging of the past to value-added, ecosystem-based community forestry. Under the Nisga'a treaty, this transition will take at least six years.

Nisga'a and non-Nisga'a hunters will share wildlife harvests. The treaty includes provisions for joint management of wildlife in two-thirds of the Nass drainage. It also contains detailed arrangements for Nisga'a rights to harvest salmon, shellfish, and other fish. Canada's Minister of Fisheries will establish the amount of the fish harvest, based on escapement runs.

Nisga'a government will be able to pass laws respecting environmental protection on Nisga'a Land as long as the laws are consistent with federal and provincial laws. This is a no-lose proposition for environmental protection on Nisga'a lands, because Nisga'a environmental management must meet the minimum standards of existing management by the provincial and federal governments.

Included in the treaty settlement is a cash payment of $190 million to the 5,500-member Nisga'a nation from the federal and provincial governments. To put this payment into perspective, it is less than the $262 million estimated cost of forest restoration for the Nisga'a territory and less than a quarter of the $826 million the BC government spent to bail out Skeena Cellulose and its 2,500 employees between 1997 and 1999. (Much of the wood supply for Skeena Cellulose has come from Nisga'a territory.)

The BC Legislature ratified the Nisga'a Final Agreement in April 1999, but as late as July 1999 the federal government had still not ratified it. To its credit, the NDP provincial government argued strongly for ratification of the treaty. But the more conservative provincial Liberal and Reform opposition parties opposed the treaty and called for a province-wide referendum on the issue. Ratification of the Nisga'a treaty is enormously important because it will serve as a model for resolving other land claims across Canada.

The Nisga'a people have extremely high unemployment and underemployment rates. Jobs in the Nisga'a communities have been mostly limited to logging, commercial fishing, seasonal mushroom harvesting, and projects initiated by the band councils and the Tribal Council. A few people also work as seasonal park rangers and tourism guides. Although some members of the Nisga'a nation have been successful as commercial fishermen and logging contractors, a large part of the population relies on various forms of social assistance and government-sponsored make-work projects. The economic development challenge for the Nisga'a people is considerable, given the distance from large urban centers where most jobs are created today.

My work with the Nisga'a began during 1992 with an assignment to prepare a master plan for the newly created Nisga'a Memorial Lava Bed park, the first provincial park in BC to be co-managed by BC Parks and a First Nation. I reported to a joint management committee composed of BC Parks representatives and a majority of Nisga'a representatives, including chairman Chief Harry Nyce. To do the necessary field work, I hired Nisga'a park ranger Charles McKay to work with me. Charles served as a guide to the park and surrounding area and was indispensable as a liaison with the Nisga'a communities.

The park master-planning process proceeded extremely well under the leadership of the Nisga'a people and was adopted by the Nisga'a nation and the BC government in 1996. The park master plan (Copeland 1993) gives prominence to the rich culture of the Nisga'a people, who welcome visitors to their aboriginal territory to share their culture and learn about traditional Nisga'a sustainable management practices. A trail to the volcanic cone area has already been constructed, and Nisga'a guides have been offering guided tours to the area. To protect this area, visitors are not allowed to visit the sensitive cone area without a guide.

Shortly after the completion of the park master plan, Charles McKay was elected to represent the Terrace Local (Nisga'a people living in the nearby City of Terrace) on the Nisga'a Tribal Council. Among other things, Charles was assigned the task of undertaking a tourism study of traditional Nisga'a territory. So I ended up working for Charles on the tourism study. Charles, Collier Azak, Bert Azak, and I spent a large part of the summer of 1993 exploring the vast Nisga'a traditional territory to evaluate the potential for tourism development. The Nisga'a Tourism Study (Copeland 1994) provided an objective evaluation of potential tourism development sites based on our extensive reconnaissance by boat, truck, and aircraft.

Nisga'a territory contains an unusually diverse and scenic combination of landscapes, seascapes, and riverine environments. These include scenic Observatory Inlet, the most remote part of the BC coast; the Nass River and its tributaries, which are suitable for guided jet boat and rafting tours and fresh water fishing; the Portland Inlet area, which offers good salt water fishing; and several beautiful remote alpine lakes which are accessible by float plane. The Nisga'a culture and history are also of great interest to visitors, particularly the choreographed Nisga'a dances with drummers and singers which tell of the Nisga'a origins, the eruption of the Wilksi baxhl mihl volcano and lava flow some 220 years ago that killed approximately 2,000 Nisga'a, and other Nisga'a stories.

While work progressed on the park master plan and the tourism study, the Nisga'a leaders were immersed in the process of negotiating the land claims settlement. To insure that the Nisga'a would be able to develop back-country tourism, the land claims settlement identified 15 sites for remote lodges and huts.

The components of the settlement also included a commercial recreation tenure and a guide-outfitting territory.

The next step was to prepare a management plan for the Nisga'a Commercial Recreation Project (Copeland 1996,1998). The plan provides the tenure necessary for the development of trails and other infrastructure on Crown land located within traditional Nisga'a territory but outside Nisga'a Land.

The number of persons employed by the Nisga'a Commercial Recreation Project is expected to increase from nine during the first year of operation to 16 in the third year, about 25 during the fifth year, and approximately 40 by the eighth year. Most of these jobs will be guides, hut keepers, and chefs. The jobs will provide much needed local employment but most importantly, they are jobs that fit well with Nisga'a aspirations. Some of the Nisga'a people have already taken tourism courses and are continuing to develop the necessary skills to become involved as guides and tourism entrepreneurs.

Closely coupled with the commercial recreation development will be an expansion of existing Nisga'a guided hiking tours in the park, boat tours on the Nass River adjacent to the park, freshwater and saltwater fishing, and the development of a Nisga'a cultural center featuring a performing arts auditorium for Nisga'a dance performances. The Nisga'a already operate saltwater fishing services from a barge which has been converted into a floating lodge. The recreation project also includes expansion of the existing Nisga'a bed-and-breakfast establishments and the development of at least one quality restaurant featuring indigenous Nisga'a food. These additional tourism development projects will substantially increase the number of tourism jobs.

The proposed Nisga'a tourism development has the potential to become a model community-based economic development project. It will be completely under the control of the Nisga'a Nation and will provide employment for local Nisga'a residents in the kind of activities they prefer. The project will be relatively environmentally benign and will eventually generate a reasonable return on Nisga'a investment. The Nisga'a have decided that their commercial recreation development is an excellent way to diversify their employment opportunities.

For an understanding of the context of the land claims settlement please read the following speech that Chief Joseph Gosnell, President of the Nisga'a Tribal Council, made to the BC Legislative Assembly in December 1998.

"Madame Speaker, today, I believe, marks a turning point in the history of British Columbia. Today aboriginal and nonaboriginal people are coming together to decide the future of this province. I am talking about the Nisga'a treaty - a triumph, I believe, for all British Columbians and a beacon of hope for aboriginal people around the world.

Nisga'a park ranger Charles McKay and tree cast on lava bed,
Nisga'a Memorial Lava Bed Provincial Park.

It's a triumph, I believe, which proves to the world that reasonable people can sit down and settle historical wrongs. It proves that a modern society can correct the mistakes of the past. As British Columbians, as Canadians, I believe we should all be very proud. It's a triumph because under the treaty, the Nisga'a people will join Canada and British Columbia as free citizens, full and equal participants in the social, economic and political life of this province and, indeed, of this county. It's a triumph because under the treaty, we will no longer be wards of the state, no longer beggars in our own land. It's a triumph because under the treaty, we will collectively own approximately 2,000 square kilometers of land, far exceeding the postage-stamp reserves set aside for us by colonial governments. We will once again govern ourselves by our own institutions but within the context of Canadian law. It is a triumph because under the treaty, we will be allowed to make our own mistakes, to savor our own victories, to stand on our own feet once again. It's a triumph because clause by clause, the Nisga'a treaty emphasizes self-reliance, personal responsibility and modern education. It also encourages, for the first time, investment in Nisga'a lands and resources and allows us to pursue meaningful employment for our own people from the resources of our own territory.

To investors, it provides economic certainty, and it gives us a fighting chance to establish legitimate economic independence, to prosper in common with our non-

Volcanic cone in Nisga'a Memorial Lava Bed Provincial Park.

aboriginal neighbors in a new and, hopefully, proud Canada. It's a triumph, Madam Speaker and honorable members, because the treaty proves beyond all doubt that negotiations – not lawsuits, not blockades, not violence – are the most effective, honorable way to resolve aboriginal issues in this country. It's a triumph, I believe, that signals the end of the Indian Act, the end of more than a century of humiliation, degradation and despair for the Nisga'a Nation.

In 1887 my ancestors made an epic journey from the Nass River to here, Victoria's Inner Harbor. Determined to settle the land question, they were met by a Premier who barred them from this Legislature. He was blunt. Premier Smithe rejected all our aspirations to settle the land question. Then he made this pronouncement: "When the white man first came among you, you were little better than wild beasts of the field. Wild beasts of the field." Little wonder, then, that this brutal racism was soon translated into narrow policies which plunged British Columbia into a century of darkness for the Nisga'a and other aboriginal people.

Like many colonists of the day, Premier Smithe did not know or care to know that the Nisga'a is an old nation – as old as any in Europe. From time immemorial, our oral literature – passed down from generation to generation – records the story of the way the Nisga'a people were placed on earth and trusted with the care and pro-

Observatory Inlet, the most remote part of the BC coast, and site of proposed Nisga'a cultural village. Observatory Inlet will serve as a key site for proposed Nisga'a marine ecotours.

tection of our land. Through the ages, we lived a settled life in villages along the Nass River. We lived in large, cedar-plank houses, fronted with totem poles depicting the great heraldry and the family crests of our nobility. We thrived from the bounty of the sea, the river, the forest and the mountains. We governed ourselves according to Ayuuk Nisga'a, the code of our own strict and ancient laws of property ownership, succession and civil order.

Between the late 1700s and mid-1800s the Nisga'a people, like so many other coastal nations of the time, as well as other tribal groups across this great land, were devastated by European diseases such as smallpox, measles and fevers. Our population, I'm told, was at one time 30,000 strong. We dwindled to about 800 people. Today I am pleased to report that our population is growing. According to our census, we now number approximately 5,500.

We took to heart the promises of King George III, set out in the Royal Proclamation of 1763, that our lands would not be taken away without our permission and that treaty-making was the way the Nisga'a would become part of this new nation. We continued to follow our Ayuuk, our code of laws. We vowed to obey the white mans law. And we expected him to obey our laws and also to respect our people.

Kinskuch Lake, site of proposed alpine cabin to be used by Nisga'a guided ecotours.

But unfortunately, the Europeans would not obey their own laws and continued to trespass on our lands. The King's governments continued to take our lands from us, until we were told that all of our land had come to belong to the Crown and that even the tiny bits of land that enclosed our villages were not ours but belonged to the government. Still we kept the faith that the rule of law would prevail one day, that justice would be done, that one day the land question would be settled fairly and honorably.

Madam Speaker, in 1913 the Nisga'a land committee drafted a petition to London. The petition contained the declaration of our traditional land ownership and governance, and it continued the critical information that in the new British colony our land ownership would be respected. In part the petition said:

"We are not opposed to the coming of the white people into our territory, provided this be carried out justly and in accordance with the British principles embodied in the Royal Proclamation. If therefore, as we expect, the aboriginal rights which we claim should be established by the decision of His Majesty's Privy Council, we would be prepared to take a moderate and reasonable position. In that event, while claiming the right to decide for ourselves the terms upon which we would deal with our territory, we would be willing that all matters outstanding between the province and ourselves should be finally adjusted by some equitable method to be

Little Amoth Lake, a subalpine/alpine site
to be utilized by proposed Nisga'a commercial recreation activities.

agreed upon, which should include representation of the Indian tribes upon any commission which might then be appointed."

The above statement was unanimously adopted at a meeting of the Nisga'a nation, or tribe of Indians, held at the village of Kincolith on the 22nd day of January, 1913. Sadly, this was not to be the case.

Also in 1913, Duncan Campbell Scott became deputy superintendent of Indian Affairs. His narrow vision of assimilation dominated federal aboriginal policy for years and years to come and was later codified as the Indian Act. Mr. Scott said: I want to get rid of the Indian problem. Our objective is to continue until there is not a single Indian in Canada that has not been absorbed into the body politic and there is no Indian question. One of this man's earliest efforts was to undermine the influence of the Nisga'a petition to London and to deflect away from political action. But these men, Smithe and Scott, failed and are now deservedly only dusty footnotes in history.

Still the situation of the Nisga'a worsened. In 1927, Canada passed a law to prevent us from pursuing our land claims, from hiring lawyers to plead our case. At the same time, our central institution of tribal government, our potlatch system we

Nisga'a singers

know in Nisga'a as ayuuk, was outlawed by an act of Parliament. It was against the law for us to give presents during our ceremonies, which is central to our tradition; our law instructs us to do that. It was made illegal for us to sing and dance, which again is a requirement of our culture. But still we did not give up and finally, under the leadership of Dr. Frank Calder, the Nisga'a Land Committee was reborn as the Nisga'a tribal council in 1955.

In 1968 we took our land question to the BC Supreme Court. We lost but appealed to the Supreme Court of Canada, where in 1973, in what is now known as the Calder case, the justice ruled that aboriginal title existed prior to Confederation. This initiated the modern-day process of land claims negotiations. The government of Canada agreed it was best to negotiate modern-day treaties. Canada agreed it was time to build a new relationship based on trust, respect and the rule of law. In time, as you will know, Madam Speaker, the province of British Columbia came to the negotiating table as well. For the past 25 years, in good faith, the Nisga'a struggled to negotiate this treaty, and finally it was initialed in August in our home community of New Aiyansh.

How the world has changed! Two days ago and 111 years later, after Smithe's rejection, I walked up to the steps of this Legislature as the sound of Nisga'a drumming

Nisga'a dancers

and singing filled the rotunda. To the Nisga'a people it was a joyous sound – the sound of freedom. Freedom is described in the dictionary as the state or condition of becoming free, the condition of not being under another's control, to say or think as one pleases. Our people have enjoyed the hospitality and the warmth of this Legislature, this capital city, its sites and its people. In churches, schools and malls, streets and public places our people have been embraced, welcomed and congratulated by the people of British Columbia.

People sometimes wonder why we have struggled so long to sign a treaty. Why, we are asked, did our elders and elected officials dedicate their lives to the resolution of the land question? What is it about a treaty?

To us a treaty is a sacred instrument. It represents an understanding between distinct cultures and shows a respect for each other's way of life. We know we are here for a long time together. A treaty stands as a symbol of high idealism in a divided world. That is why we have fought so long and so hard. I have been asked: Has this been worth it? I would have to say, with a resounding yes, it has.

But believe me and my colleagues; it has been a long, hard-fought battle for those that went before us. Some may have heard us say that a generation of Nisga'a men

Nisga'a storytelling

and women have grown old at the negotiating table. Sadly, it is very true. I was a much younger man when I began, became involved in the tribal council; I was 25 years old. Today I'm 63; my hair is graying. I've gone through six terms of Prime Ministers. I recall their names – the Rt. Hon. Pierre Trudeau, Joe Clark, John Turner, Brian Mulroney, Kim Campbell and Jean Chretien – and five British Columbia premiers – Bill Bennett, William Vander Zalm, Rita Johnson, Mike Harcourt and, yes Glen Clark. I will spare you the list of deputy ministers, senior bureaucrats and other officials. There are numerous names that we have met across these many years. Their names, I believe, would paper the walls of this chamber at least twice.

We are not naive. We know that some people do not want this treaty. We know that there are naysayers – some sitting here today. We know that there are those who say Canada and British Columbia are giving us too much, and a few who want to reopen negotiations in order to give us less. Others, still upholding the values of Smithe and Scott, are practicing willful ignorance. This colonial attitude is fanning the flames of fear and ignorance in this province and reigniting a poisonous attitude that we as aboriginal people are so familiar with.

But these are desperate tactics, doomed to fail. By playing politics with the aspirations of aboriginal peoples, these naysayers are blighting the promise of the Nisga'a treaty not only for us but for nonaboriginal people as well, because this is about people. Were not numbers. The issue that you will deal with over the next weeks...You will deal with the lives of our people, the future of our people. It is about the legitimate aspirations of our people, no longer willing to step aside or be marginalized. We intend to be free and equal citizens. Witness the flags that have been waved in this chamber of the past two days by the Nisga'a people of British Columbia, the Nisga'a people of Canada.

Now, on the eve of the fiftieth anniversary of the Declaration of Human rights, this Legislature embarks on a great debate about aboriginal rights. The Nisga'a people welcome that debate, one of the most important in the modern history of British Columbia. We have every confidence that elected members of this Legislature will look beyond narrow politics to correct the shameful and historic wrong, I ask each and every one of you, honorable members, to search your hearts deeply and to allow the light of our message to guide your decisions. We have worked for justice for more than 100 years. Now it is time to ratify the Nisga'a treaty, for aboriginal and nonaboriginal people to come together and write a new chapter in the history of our nation, our province, our country and, indeed, the world. The world, I believe, is our witness to the endeavors that we have encountered.

Madam Speaker, on behalf of the Nisga'a nation, I greatly appreciate the privilege that has been accorded to me to address this chamber. Thank you."

Chapter 12

THE HAISLA NATION
AND SAVING THE KITLOPE

This is the story of how the Haisla First Nation and Ecotrust, an environmental group based in Portland, Oregon, worked together to protect the Kitlope, the largest remaining pristine temperate rainforest watershed in the world.

The Kitlope is located within the traditional territory of the Henaaksiala people of the Haisla nation on the north coast of British Columbia at the southern end of Gardner Canal. Logging, hydroelectric generation, a pulp mill, Alcan's huge aluminum smelter, and other industrial activities have severely affected most of the traditional territory of the Haisla people. The Greater Kitlope ecosystem is the only large area within their territory that remains in pristine condition. The Haisla are extremely concerned about the future of the Kitlope and insist that they must have substantial control over everything that takes place there. They oppose "any proposals or acts that threaten the lands, waters, and living creatures of the Kitlope" and have invited others to join them "in wonder and respect for the Kitlope" (Haisla Nation Kitlope Declaration, 1991).

A comprehensive analysis of BC's remaining pristine coastal rain forest watersheds revealed that the Kitlope River watershed is the largest pristine rainforest in British Columbia (Moore 1991). This finding prompted Ecotrust and Conservation International Canada to commission a Cultural and Scientific Reconnaissance of the Greater Kitlope ecosystem during the summer of 1991 (Travers 1991). Before this field trip, official records included only eight birds and nine mammals, mostly because biologists and naturalists were not able to get access to this remote area. The list of 17 grew to 120 during the project. During this assessment, the Haisla revisited a number of traditional sites, located a number of culturally modified trees, and tentatively identified the site of a "lost" village on Kitlope Lake. The reconnaissance also carried out an on-site examination of the disputed location of an oolichan spawning bed in the immediate vicinity of a proposed log dump and booming ground. The scientific study team revealed that only three percent of the Greater Kitlope ecosystem has been classified as operable for the timber industry. They concluded that within the expansive 405,000-hectare ecosystem, prey-predator relationships still have room to function in a natural and complete way without significant interference from mankind.

The following year, the Haisla nation and Ecotrust developed a wilderness planning framework for the Greater Kitlope ecosystem (Copeland et al. 1992). I served on the planning team along with biologist Wayne McCrory, forester Ray Travers, biologist John Kelson, Haisla liaison person Delores Grant, and Ecotrust's Ken

Haisla Nana Kila pole at Kemano.

Margolis. The findings and recommendations in the study are based on the knowledge, wisdom, and enthusiastic support of the Haisla people. Elders Gordon Robertson, Cecil Paul, Alan Hall, James Robertson, and John Wilson provided a historical perspective on what the Kitlope means to the Haisla community. Chief councillor Gerald Amos and councillors Kenny Hall and Charlie Shaw were instrumental in providing the vision contained in our report. The most remarkable aspect of the Haisla input was the respect the Haisla people hold for their hereditary chiefs, who represented the highest values of their community.

During the early summer of 1992, my son Ryan and I travelled on the Greenpeace sailing ship *Rainbow Warrior* from Kitimat to the Kitlope. The ship also carried a European delegation and several Haisla members plus Chief Gerald Amos's inboard jet boat, several barrels of fuel, and other supplies. The party was transported to a Haisla camp located in the upper part of the estuary. All persons entering the Kitlope were advised to wash their faces with fresh water from the

Myron Kozak

Kitlope River.

Adrian Forsyth

*Hereditary Chief
Cecil Paul.*

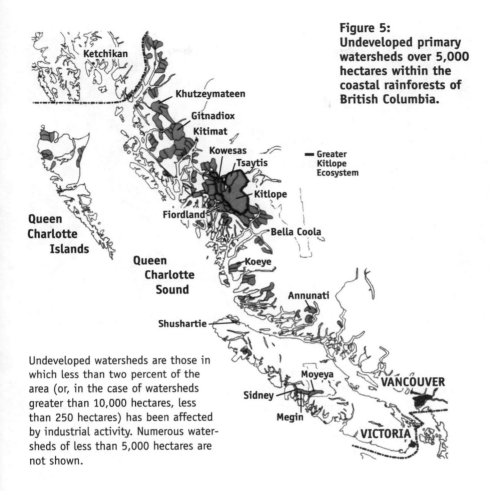

**Figure 5:
Undeveloped primary watersheds over 5,000 hectares within the coastal rainforests of British Columbia.**

Undeveloped watersheds are those in which less than two percent of the area (or, in the case of watersheds greater than 10,000 hectares, less than 250 hectares) has been affected by industrial activity. Numerous watersheds of less than 5,000 hectares are not shown.

river. According to Haisla custom, this ritual helps people see the beauty of the area. After the group departed later that day, Ryan and I began to explore the rivers of the Kitlope by inflatable jet boat. We had previously explored many wilderness areas in the province, but the Kitlope seemed to us to be the wildest place of all. We were later joined in our reconnaissance of the area by biologists John Kelson and Wayne McCrory.

While our study progressed over the spring and summer of 1992, the logging company that held the license to log the Kitlope was busy laying out their proposed roads and logging plans. At a public meeting, the company offered to hire approximately 50 Haisla workers for many years to do the logging work. These would have been high-paying jobs. In response to the company's offer, hereditary chief Cecil Paul stood up and declared that the company would have to get rid of him before any logging equipment could enter the Kitlope. All of the other Haisla

Tezwa River.

people present at the meeting supported Cecil's stand, and several of them spoke eloquently of the need to protect their ancestral homeland.

The wilderness planning framework recommended a number of permitted uses that would be compatible with the area's wilderness characteristics. These included traditional Haisla subsistence hunting and fishing, a Rediscovery Youth Camp, ecosystem research (including forest dynamics, fisheries, and other subjects), limited guided ecological and cultural tourism, and minimum-impact tourist access. Prohibited uses included commercial logging, mining, hydroelectric development, and road construction.

A board of directors would develop a management agreement and supporting policies, and a Nana-Kila Watchmen Program operating from a base station located near the head of Kitlope Lake would be responsible for enforcing the policies. The Watchmen would coordinate the activities of the proposed Rediscovery Camp, research projects, and ecotour operations. These activities were expected to create 33 full and part-time jobs by the fourth year of operation, or the equivalent of 12 full-time jobs.

Aided by substantial funding from Ecotrust, the Haisla people immediately began putting these activities in operation. A Haisla Rediscovery Camp opened during the summer of 1992. Nana-Kila Watchmen have been trained to work with BC Parks patrolling the lower parts of the Kitlope area. And visits to the area by ecotourism operators are increasing. In January 1992, representatives of the Haisla Nation and Ecotrust met with provincial cabinet ministers to open discussions on

Kitlope estuary ecosite.

protecting the area. Three months later, the Haisla conducted a workshop for government and industry representatives on the future management of the Kitlope.

In 1993, a year after publication of the Wilderness Planning Framework, the company that held rights to harvest timber in the Kitlope (West Fraser) voluntarily relinquished its cutting rights so that the conservancy could be established. In August 1994, the BC government and the Haisla nation announced that the Kitlope would be fully protected and the Haisla nation and BC Parks would be jointly responsible for managing it. In February 1996, the Huchsduwachsdu Nuyem Jees/Kitlope Heritage Conservancy was established by Order-in-Council. At the same time, the Haisla nation and the BC government signed an agreement to manage the conservancy jointly and to establish a Kitlope Management Committee. The committee is composed of three members appointed by the Haisla nation, three members appointed by the BC government, and a mutually chosen chair. The Kitlope Management Committee is currently in the process of developing a comprehensive management plan for the Kitlope. The conservancy is operated by BC Parks, which has contracted with the Nana-Kila Institute to provide a watchman/ranger service. During the summer of 1998, former chief councillor Gerald Amos and Bruce Hill commenced operation of guided ecotours into the Kitlope. Several other ecotour companies have also started operations in the watershed. All commercial tour groups provide Haisla interpretive guides.

Because saving the Kitlope has more than local significance, the partnership between the Haisla nation and BC Parks makes sense. It blends issues of international significance with an indigenous community's local control of land use. The local community drove the process of protecting the Kitlope. Without the community's high level of spiritual energy related to the place and their culture and their enthusiastic support for preserving the Kitlope, protection of the area would not have been possible.

The Kitlope is a model success story of a First Nation, an environmental group, a logging company, and government coming together to accomplish a major shift in the management of an area with international significance as well as great value to a local community. The cultural heritage of the Haisla Nation and the ecological integrity of the world's largest remaining temperate rainforest have been preserved. This momentous event has created substantial opportunities for economic diversification and new job creation for the Haisla community.

Acts of Balance
Part 5:

INTEGRATING THE
GLOBAL WITH THE LOCAL

Overview

Previous chapters advocated the benefits of community economic development because community-based development is necessary for global survival and sustainability and preferable to control of local resources by a global economy. But there are exceptions when green products require the kind of research, development, and production resources that transcend the capacity of enterprises that are community-based and community-controlled.

Whether we like it or not, we are now in the information age. We are also in a period of unprecedented technological development and change in business management methods. Computers, the internet, and robotics are here to stay because they offer more efficient and cost-effective ways to get things done. Some advantages of technology extend to community-based development and the environmental movement. These include global communication, saving paper, and using robotics to handle hazardous production processes. However, developing and marketing complex technology usually requires the resources of a large corporation.

Today, large companies such as Microsoft dominate the production of software. Despite the fact that large companies such as IBM and Apple dominate retail sales of computers, Intel's development of a central processing unit (CPU) quickly established a virtual global monopoly in the production of these units. Within a very short period of time, most of the leading computer manufacturers were using this processor technology. Unless other manufacturers can match the virtues of the Intel Pentium processor, they will inevitably face difficulties marketing inferior products.

Nevertheless, many community-based companies fulfill niches in the computer and software market. Local servers provide essential links to the worldwide web and often design web sites and CD ROMs for local companies. Other operators work from home, producing after-market products and custom engineering components and processes for larger companies and markets located in far away cities and countries. Many of these home-based businesses have been made possible by the advanced communications technology of modems, powerful but inexpensive computers, and the internet. Marketing through the internet is growing rapidly. Last year Retallack Resort (Chapter 5) received more inquiries from its new web site than from any other form of advertising. Today, even small community-based businesses must use this technology to market their products successfully and keep up-to-date with rapidly evolving technological developments around the world.

There is a challenge here. How can we justify and support the need for economic development that transcends the limitations of community-based production? Where do we draw the line between supporting larger projects and opposing them? This depends to a large extent on how environmentally benign and socially acceptable the products are, and where the resources will come from to finance the substantial research and development required by innovation.

Competing land uses also need to be factored into the evaluation of projects that involve the use of Crown land. In the development of the Retallack Resort, gladed ski runs and carefully managed selective logging are less damaging to the environment than clearcut logging. In the Kitlope, ecotourism is more ecologically and culturally acceptable than industrial logging and mining.

The two case studies in this section represent relatively green companies that are in the process of developing and producing complicated high-tech products. These are Ballard Power, which is leading the world in the development of fuel cell technology, and Hydroxyl, a smaller company that is producing state-of-the-art sewage disposal systems.

Chapter 13

BALLARD AND HYDROXYL: ACCOMMODATING HIGH TECH

The Ballard Fuel Cell

The largest source of air pollution in the world comes from burning fossil fuels in stationary power plants and in cars, trucks, busses, trains, and airplanes. A more ecologically sound alternative is the fuel cell. Ballard Power Systems of Burnaby, BC, is the current leader in developing this technology.

Fuel cells are electrochemical devices that are clean, quiet, and efficient. Because fuel cells have no moving parts, they have excellent reliability and long operating lives. Fuel cell systems can use many different fuels without combustion, including natural gas, methanol, gasoline, and hydrogen. Ballard's fuel cells have a high enough power density (power related to size) to operate an automobile and the refuelling ease of an internal combustion engine. Fuel cell systems feature the positive qualities of internal combustion engines and batteries without the negative attributes of either.

Fuel cell technology has been around for several decades; NASA used fuel cells as a power source in the US space program during the 1960s. But it has been too expensive for most other applications. Ballard Power Systems has been working on the development of fuel cells for automotive applications and stationary power plants since 1983. The research and development costs of this technology have already reached the billions. In May 1999 the company was worth approximately $4.5 billion on the Toronto Stock Exchange. This is nearly twice as much as MacMillan Bloedel. Stock in Ballard Power has produced some of the highest gains on the stock market during the past three years. Ballard's clients include General Motors, Nissan, Honda, Mazda, Volkswagen and Volvo, Daimler-Chrysler, Ford, and other companies interested in stationary and portable power plants.

Several buses powered by Ballard fuel cells have been successfully operating in Chicago in the US and in Vancouver in Canada. Ballard is currently producing and selling 250-kilowatt stationary fuel cell power plants for buildings and other applications. But the biggest potential market for fuel cells is passenger cars. Private automobiles are not an ecologically friendly form of urban transportation because they contribute to urban sprawl and the construction of extensive systems of paved roads and parking lots. However, nonpolluting fuel cells are much preferable to internal combustion engines in all forms of transportation.

Cars powered by fuel cells drive like normal automobiles, but fuel cells produce no pollutants in the process of converting hydrogen and oxygen into electrical

Buses powered by fuel cells have operated in Chicago since 1998.

power. There is no combustion. Fuel cells leave a trail of water vapor instead of carbon dioxide, nitrous oxide, and other pollutants. California has established a standard of zero emissions from 10 per cent of cars sold in the state by 2003. This standard has spurred fuel-cell development.

Fuel cells operate most efficiently on liquid hydrogen fuel. This fuel can be obtained, for example, through hydroelectric generation or by converting natural gas or methane to hydrogen. In the US Pacific northwest and Canada, surplus hydroelectric energy is wasted during spring runoff. This surplus could be used to produce liquid hydrogen fuel. One example would be to produce hydrogen from surplus hydroelectric power and/or power supplied from Grand Coulee Dam in Washington State under the newly negotiated Columbia River Treaty. It would be possible to store this energy and transport it by pipeline or truck it to metropolitan areas where it could be dispensed to automobile, bus, and truck fleets and private car owners.

One primary reason for Ballard's success as the world's leading developer of fuel cell technology is its partnership with two of the world's largest auto manufacturers, Daimler-Chrysler and Ford. Each of these companies has invested approximately $500 million in Ballard, and Daimler has put some of its top production engineers in Burnaby to help Ballard develop a financially feasible process for mass production of fuel cells. Mercedes-Benz recently rolled out a compact car powered by Ballard fuel cells that seats five, has a 450-kilometer range and can do 150 km/h. However, this concept car, the NECAR 4, is still far from reaching the market. Its fuel is liquid hydrogen, it weighs 500 kilograms more than an equivalent gasoline-powered car, and mass production of its fuel cell hardware would cost at least $30,000 US per car. But it was billed as a significant gain for Daimler-Chrysler in the competition among auto makers to sell zero-emission vehicles by

Mercedes Benz prototype fuel-cell-powered car.

2003. Ford – which owns 15 percent of Ballard – demonstrated a version of its five-seat fuel-cell-powered car, the P2000, during the spring of 1999. Ford is working on developing the electric drive components that are necessary for fuel-cell-powered vehicles.

It is possible that Ballard has started a revolution in the vertical hierarchy of auto manufacturing, in which the manufacturer is at the top and component manufacturers are subordinate. If a newcomer from outside the industry such as Ballard can set an industry standard in the core component of an automobile, the engine, then the same company may be able to be a price leader. Such a company could occupy the same monopoly position as Intel (Nikkei Business Magazine 1998). A University of British Columbia commerce professor noted in a local TV interview that if BC could capture only ten percent of the world's future demand for fuel cell engines, it could generate more revenue and exports than BC's entire forest industry.

The level of investment required to attempt Ballard's objectives is a significant factor. The demands of Ballard's research and development work go beyond the ability of most Canadian companies to find capital and expertise. Yet the product is highly advanced from an environmental point of view. The environmental movement and both the Canadian and British Columbia governments could support the company. Governments could assist by funding basic research in fuel cells, converting their fleets of busses to run on fuel cell power, and helping with generating, storing, and transporting hydrogen fuel. Investing several hundred million in Ballard's fuel cell technology makes much better economic sense than bailing out BC's antiquated pulp mills.

Ballard's fuel cell development is a good example of an environmentally benign

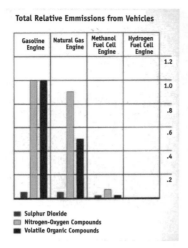

Total Relative Emmissions from Vehicles

Gasoline Engine	Natural Gas Engine	Methanol Fuel Cell Engine	Hydrogen Fuel Cell Engine

- ■ Sulphur Dioxide
- ▨ Nitrogen-Oxygen Compounds
- ■ Volatile Organic Compounds

Above: Ballard 250 kilowatt stationary power plant.

Left: Emmissions from hydrogen fuel are much less than from gasoline, natural gas or methanol.

product that requires substantial investment in research and development. As an example of ecological economics, fuel cell technology contains contradictions such as the continued use of cars in metropolitan areas and the size of the investment, which greatly exceeds the financial capacities of community-based economic development. However, the product Ballard intends to mass produce will most likely create more environmental benefits than costs in the foreseeable future. The world is a complicated place, and there will always be contradictions and the need for imperfect solutions.

Hydroxyl Advanced Wastewater Systems

Hydroxyl Systems is based in Sidney, BC. The company designs and builds advanced water and wastewater treatment systems and nonhazardous liquid waste processing facilities. Hydroxyl's modular wastewater treatment plants are ideal for residential, commercial, and recreational applications. The plants combine superior aerobic and anoxic biological processes with Hydroxyl's advanced oxidation processes in a self-contained, weatherproof, remote-monitored module, well suited for multiphase developments. This technology dispenses with the need for soil to further "treat" the effluent. If the effluent is discharged into the soil, it takes a smaller land area compared with conventional package treatment plant systems. This can make a big difference to high density projects built on expensive land where there are no sewers (Hydroxyl Systems 1998).

Renovated water from this system has been used to supplement stream flows. The system also contributes to water conservation and saves money, because the effluent can be reused for subsurface irrigation and toilet flushing. It is possible to phase in this high-tech system for quality tertiary sewage treatment or expand it as required for successive stages of the project. The company provides operating, maintenance, and in-house engineering services for its clients in Canada and the United States.

Hydroxyl sewage wastewater treatment systems have been successfully installed and operated in public schools, shopping centers, remote recreation facilities in national parks, housing developments, and marine applications in the United States and Canada.

Sewage treatment plants are under increasing pressure to produce clean, disinfected effluent for reuse applications such as irrigation. In addition, there are numerous safety issues associated with the handling of chlorine liquid or gas and adverse environmental effects caused by chlorine, chlorides, and trihalomethanes. Costs associated with dechlorination have prompted many wastewater treatment plants and agencies to explore and evaluate alternate methods of effluent disinfection.

Hydroxyl also engineers and produces equipment for industrial wastewater solutions, biosolids processing, and recycling systems. Hydroxyl's biosolids recovery techniques can remove and treat the solid component of septage sludge and other nonhazardous solids and convert them to a high-quality approved soil conditioner and fertilizer suitable for agricultural and horticultural applications.

Hydroxyl Systems provides alternative cost-effective technologies for potable water treatment, including positive flotation mechanisms for removing suspended solids and ozone and advanced oxidation processes for destroying water-soluble organic substances. The process achieves primary disinfection without chlorination, which reduces the byproducts of disinfection dramatically. The Hydroxyl technology removes high color, iron and manganese, the organisms giardia and cryptosporidium, and suspended solids in order to meet drinking water standards. The company's laboratory and production facilities in Sidney, BC, provide biological testing. Hydroxyl has also worked with the Canadian government on the development of advanced treatment technologies.

There is a major problem with implementation of innovative solutions to our environmental problems – acceptance and approval by health inspectors. In the small village of New Denver, BC, a developer tried to get approval to use a Hydroxyl sewage treatment system for a small project of about a dozen residential and commercial buildings. The project is located close to Lake Slocan and the village's backup water pump. The village of New Denver does not provide sewer services, and the community has depended on conventional septic tank/drain field systems, which require large land areas. The health inspector refused the application to use the new technology without reserving enough land for a conventional drain field as a backup system. If the developer were required to provide the land for a conventional backup system, the new technology would offer no advantage.

Our system for regulating sewage disposal is dysfunctional on some levels and over-restrictive on other levels. It is puzzling that we continue to allow people to occupy existing residences with no septic tanks or drain fields. Allowing this indefinitely is environmentally unsound, since dumping untreated sewage directly into the ground can cause detrimental effects on neighboring properties and common watercourses. In Victoria, BC, huge amounts of raw sewage are dumped into Juan de Fuca Strait every day. Similar situations exist in the Vancouver area.

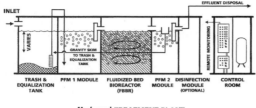

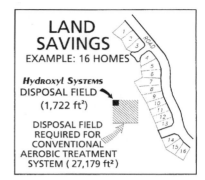

Hydroxyl TREATMENT PLANT
(IN OR ABOVE GROUND): SCHEMATIC SECTION

Hydroxyl treatment plant (above) can result in significant reduction in the amount of land necessary for sewage disposal (right).

LAND SAVINGS
EXAMPLE: 16 HOMES

Hydroxyl Systems
DISPOSAL FIELD
(1,722 ft²)

DISPOSAL FIELD
REQUIRED FOR
CONVENTIONAL
AEROBIC TREATMENT
SYSTEM (27,179 ft²)

Governments allow themselves to pollute our waterways, yet health inspectors refuse to accept new, nonpolluting technology when developers propose to use it.

In some applications, Hydroxyl Systems has successfully installed and operated their system despite many of these institutional and bureaucratic constraints, but success has usually required sustained effort on the part of developers and the company's engineers. The government's dismal regulatory system needs to be revised. Governments could encourage innovative solutions to environmental problems and lead the way by using these new systems in public projects which they manage. As a matter of principle, it makes sense for governments to rectify the inadequacy of huge public sewage disposal systems before they regulate developers of much smaller projects, especially when developers propose to use advanced and proven technology. In addition, governments could accelerate their assistance with the research and development of innovative solutions.

Hydroxyl is a relatively small company and perhaps partly because of its size, the company has encountered slow government acceptance of its products in some jurisdictions. Larger companies usually have more clout with government regulators because they can invest time and money to retain persuasive lawyers and specialized engineering expertise to win government acceptance. This advantage is inequitable to smaller business operators. Hydroxyl has proven the effectiveness of its products. Health inspectors and government engineers have been given the responsibility to learn about and approve advanced proven technology without undue delay and resistance.

Ballard's fuel cell and Hydroxyl's wastewater systems represent exceptions to the usual advantages of community-based economic development. Although their ownership and development are not community-based, these technologies offer ecologically superior methods of providing power and disposing of sewage. A small community cannot provide the kind of resources this kind of technological research and development requires.

**Acts of Balance
Part 6:**

GOVERNMENT:
MAKING THE DIFFERENCE

Overview

There is a lot governments could do to improve the regulatory processes through which they manage our economic affairs. In the intermediate time frame, the most pressing need is to reduce the size of government subsidies for the ecologically and economically unsustainable and now declining forest, mining, and fishing industries. The subsidies give these large industries an unfair advantage at the same time that provincial and federal governments are overtaxing and over-regulating the smaller, up-and-coming and more promising segments of the economy in the Pacific northwest.

Governments could reduce unnecessary red tape and bureaucratic interference in small business operations by developing better methods of coordinating the activities of government departments and agencies. A coordinated effort to encourage community-based economic development and preserve cultural, biological, and economic diversity would support innovative and creative project initiatives that are appropriate environmentally, socially, and economically. Unless our governments make these crucially important changes, our local, regional, and national economies will, by default, fall further into the black hole of rapidly increasing globalization. This book describes several experiences in the Pacific northwest which demonstrate that communities can adapt to evolving economic conditions much more easily than industry and government economists have predicted.

This section does not offer a panacea for solving these problems, only a few suggestions, such as changing the building inspection process, developing a one-stop coordinated project approval process, eliminating perverse subsidies to the forest industry, and increasing public support for parks, trails, and public transit. This section suggests a few guidelines governments could use to evaluate and support innovative economic development projects.

Chapter 14

RED TAPE: REMOVING THE BARRIERS

Building Inspection

Nearly everyone I have interviewed who is involved in building projects has questioned the usefulness of the present mandatory and extremely complex building code and the often onerous interpretations of the code by building inspectors. The recent leaky condominium issue in Vancouver, BC, illustrates that the code and the system of building inspections often fail to protect property owners and apartment tenants. Governments rarely fix problems that building inspectors miss.

Many governments don't like the legal liability that goes with responsibility for enforcing complex building codes. After being forced to pay court costs and damages as a result of faulty building inspection, the Regional District of Central Kootenay applied to the British Columbia government for permission to drop the function of building inspection. Many smaller villages and towns do not want this responsibility. The BC government has repeatedly rejected the Regional District's request to drop the building inspection function, even though other jurisdictions in the province are not required to provide this service.

Most architects, engineers, and building contractors agree that the BC Building Code has become far too complex and difficult to understand. The code's priority is fire protection. But architects, engineers, and their clients have found that the code is far too inflexible to accommodate aesthetic and economic considerations. The building inspection process has also become extremely expensive. The building permit for Retallack Lodge (see Chapter 5) was $9,000; the building permit for my own modest 1,500-square-foot timber-frame home was $900. Most building inspectors have no training in architecture or engineering. Although some of them are experienced tradespersons, all they have to do to qualify as building inspectors is pass a test on the building code.

Professional architects and structural and mechanical engineers, on the other hand, must graduate from university programs, serve an apprenticeship, and then pass a comprehensive examination on their professional skills. These are the people who should be responsible for the design and construction processes because they are the most qualified. When their work fails, they should be accountable and should have to pay the consequences. The building inspection process has been superimposed on professional responsibilities, and building inspectors frequently override the designs and specifications of professional architects and engineers. This happened many times during the design, engineering, and construction of Retallack Lodge.

People who have not been involved in the process of construction may be concerned that, without the existing building inspection process, they would have no way of knowing whether or not a building is safe to occupy. A less expensive option would be to hire qualified and experienced professionals or tradespersons to inspect a property before buying it. These inspectors could be trained engineers, architects, or experienced builders. A building survey could be similar to a marine survey in which prospective purchasers hire qualified professionals to assess a boat's quality and safety. This is an important distinction; a marine surveyor works for the prospective buyer. If building assessments were conducted in this way, they would be more up-to-date than they are under the present practice of building inspection, which occurs only at the time of construction. In Vancouver, BC, prospective condominium buyers are commissioning inspections from knowledgeable professionals.

In addition to building inspectors, the present building code provides for legal specialists who are licensed to certify that changes from the code meet the intent of the code. But these special code interpreters are extremely expensive to hire, and most small builders and contractors either don't know about them or can't afford them, especially in the more remote parts of the province. In most cases, these specialists have worked on large multimillion dollar urban commercial and industrial projects where the cost of their services is more affordable.

In my view, the present building permit system is costly and unnecessary and needs serious reform. The building code and its detailed provisions should be merely guidelines. This would give professionals the flexibility they need to integrate aesthetic and economic considerations into their designs. Professionals are qualified to design and engineer buildings without the aid of building inspectors and regulations.

One-Stop Evaluation

Government employees have a propensity to avoid and/or postpone decision making, especially when a decision involves several departments or agencies. A lack of clear government policy makes this propensity even worse. For most development projects, approvals should take no more than a few months – or for larger projects or projects that have more than local significance and impact, a year at most.

In BC, part of the reason for the delays in approving new developments has been the lack of a definitive land-use policy that cuts across the various ministries and levels of government that are involved. Another reason is the tendency for government employees to avoid responsibility for these decisions in the absence of such a policy. Developers often hear the excuse that there are not enough government staff to regulate land use. In fact, there are too many levels of supervision and authority and too few persons to do the work in the field. Rapid turnover and transfer of government staff make this situation worse. In the present system, it can be very difficult to identify who is responsible for making decisions.

Using quasi-judicial procedures to evaluate larger projects would ensure that these projects get a fair hearing and would result in speedier and more responsible decisions. In this process, all affected agencies and members of the public would have two to three months to respond to a development proposal in writing or at a public hearing. To developers and entrepreneurs, time is money; they cannot wait forever. If the approval process is unduly long, they will probably look elsewhere for opportunities. This is one reason why many BC entrepreneurs and companies have moved to Alberta and Washington State.

The smaller the project, the more onerous the effect of delays in approvals will be and the more likely developers will be discouraged from undertaking such projects. Retallack Resort spent approximately $200,000, or about ten percent of the total initial development cost, in the process of obtaining operating permits. This and other factors related to over-regulation and excessive taxation of the project make it unlikely that most shareholders of that company would attempt such a project again. Failure to reward entrepreneurial initiative is a huge obstacle to the formation of new businesses and the diversification and evolution of the economy.

In a one-stop approval process, all government agencies and members of the public would have a chance to comment on a proposed land-use project at a hearing before a trained and impartial examiner. In Washington State, the examiners are usually persons with a masters degree in planning, some training in land-use law, and at least several years experience working with government on land-use planning and management. Others are lawyers with training and experience in land-use planning. Hearing examiners act as judges and must be extremely impartial. Usually, they do not meet privately with the developer or government agents before a hearing. Although the use of hearing examiners is not mandated under Washington State legislation, many city and county councils in Washington State employ the services of hearing examiners. In these jurisdictions, elected representatives focus on making policy and leave most of the administration of these policies to their hearing examiners and planning staff.

In a one-stop process, government agencies, the developer, and public interest groups would benefit from working together to achieve a balanced overall solution before any public hearing takes place. If they are unable to arrive at an agreed solution, the hearing examiner would make the decision after reviewing government policies and hearing all the evidence and submissions.

The Washington State Land Planning Commission recommended this one-stop hearing process as part of a comprehensive land-use bill in 1972 (Substitute House Bill 791 or HB 791). The one-stop, hearing-examiner system was designed to promote fair consideration of development proposals within reasonable time limits. It also would have created a more efficient and better-focused process for arriving at decisions on land and resource-use issues.

Environmental groups and developers both supported the Washington State Land Planning Commission's proposal, and the legislation passed with a two-thirds majority in the House of Representatives and the strong support of the Governor. Developers supported the legislation because they wanted a speedier and less expensive system of granting development permits. Environmental groups supported the bill because it mandated environmental planning at all levels of government, from the state level down to regional and county levels and municipalities. The bill specified a method for determining the carrying capacity of the land in higher-level planning processes, particularly at the state level. The Washington State Land Planning Commission worked for nearly two years on the development of HB 791 and spent over half-a-million dollars in the process.

Despite this broad-based support, the chairman of the Washington Senate Committee on State Government effectively vetoed the proposed legislation by not scheduling consideration of the bill before his committee. How could this happen when the bill had so much support? Although there is no clear answer, one reason stems from the structure of the legislative process in the US, with its strong system of checks and balances. In the US, it often happens that one of the two legislative bodies at the state or federal level rejects a bill that the other legislative body supports. Other bills are vetoed at the committee level, and sometimes, as with HB 791, a committee chairman simply rejects or ignores them. The chairman of this Senate committee was diametrically opposed to land-use planning. This is why committee chairs can be so powerful in the US. Compared to the multiple veto system in the US, the Canadian parliamentary form of government seems simple. If the party in power has a majority of votes, it can always pass a piece of legislation, or the cabinet can issue an order-in-council, which does not require legislative action. The downside to the Canadian system is that it is nearly impossible to make a change in policy when the party in power opposes it.

Regardless of the political system involved, one key to making land-use decisions more efficiently is to establish clear public policy and guidelines for land-use development. The clearer the policy and guidelines, the easier the decision-making process will be for the government agents and hearing examiners who administer the process. The lack of clear public policy, comprehensive land-use plans, and economic strategies hampers development, especially the kind of community-based economic development that usually involves smaller operators. The lack of clear but flexible policy and performance standards also hinders more innovative projects.

Instead of acting as a regulator, governments could provide more positive encouragement and support of appropriate types of community-based economic development. This level of involvement would operate more like a partnership; government representatives would be functioning in a help mode in the approval and implementation phases of developments that meet established policy and criteria.

Chapter 15

PERVERSE SUBSIDIES: ELIMINATE THEM!

"The law doth lock up both man and woman, who steals the goose from off the common, but lets the greater felon loose, who steals the common from the goose."
Anonymous, circa 16th century

"Corporate economists treat as free commodities not only the air, water, and soil, but also the delicate web of social relations, which is severely affected by continuing economic expansion. Private profits are being made at the expense of public costs in the deterioration of the environment and the general quality of life, and at the expense of future generations. The market place simply gives us the wrong information. There is a lack of feedback, and basic ecological literacy tells us that such a system is not sustainable."
Fritjof Capra, 1996

A study by Norman Myers, an honorary fellow at Green College in Oxford University, estimates that the governments of the world spend $1.9 trillion US per year to subsidize agriculture, fossil fuels, nuclear energy, road transportation, water, and fisheries and that perverse subsidies amount to a further $1.45 trillion US annually. Total government subsidies come to a staggering $3.35 trillion US. This is twice as much all the world's governments spend on their military budgets every year. By "perverse" Myers means bad for the environment and the economy. Perverse subsidies increase governments' costs and budget deficits and lead to higher taxes and higher prices. According to Myers, reducing the amount of perverse subsidies by half would enable many governments to abolish their budget deficits and safeguard their environments (Myers and Kent 1998).[3]

Myers has established that the overall costs of the car culture in the United Kingdom totals $117 billion per year. These costs include pollution, congestion, and accidents. Taxpayers and every citizen who suffers from the effects of the car culture bear these costs. Germany spends $4 billion US a year to support its coal mining industry, or $50,000 US per miner per year. According to Myers, both the German economy and the environment would benefit if the government closed all of the country's coal mines, sent the miners home, and paid them full wages for the rest of their lives. Although the Canadian government subsidized the Hibernia oil platform in Newfoundland by at least $1 billion, the project has not made any

---

3: Unless indicated otherwise, figures are in Canadian dollars. Although currency exchange rates vary over time, to convert Canadian dollars to US dollars, divide the number of Canadian dollars by 1.47. To convert Canadian dollars to British pounds sterling, divide Canadian dollars by 2.34.

money, and Mobil Oil has pulled out of the consortium. Canadian taxpayers have also been subsidizing the Canadian nuclear power industry by at least $100 million annually for years. And these subsidies pale in comparison with subsidies to the petroleum and automotive industries in support of North America's car culture.

Government subsidies make up the gap between the selling price of the annual world catch of fish ($80 billion US) and the catch's actual dockside worth ($100 billion US). This subsidy, which organizations as diverse as the United Nations Food and Agriculture Organization and the World Wildlife Fund have documented, has encouraged overfishing to the point where commercial fisheries are almost extinct. The depletion of fish stocks has led to bankruptcies and increased unemployment for fishermen.

In Britain, Myers found that the taxpayer forks out a least $819 per year for agricultural subsidies, an additional $468 per year in increased food prices, plus environmental costs such as pollution of water supplies through pesticide and fertilizer wash-off and degraded landscapes. Restricting production keeps prices artificially high; this benefits farmers, but raises costs to consumers. In many countries of the world, agricultural subsidies are huge. In the US, many farmers are paid not to grow crops on part or all of their prime agricultural land.

Elimination of subsidies does not necessarily mean the demise of industrial and commercial activities. New Zealand, for instance, has eliminated most of its agricultural subsidies; yet its agricultural industry is more successful than ever and has generated increased employment in farming.

The political climate for reducing these subsidies is propitious. As more governments emphasize the free market and private enterprise, there is growing pressure to reduce government intervention and spending. According to Myers, "India's subsidies total over fourteen percent of gross domestic product, but the new government wants to reduce its fiscal deficit to under four percent. Russia reduced its fossil-fuel subsidies from $29 billion US in 1990-91 to $9 billion US in 1995-96; China from $25 billion US to $10 billion US. Several Latin American countries, notably Chile and Argentina, have started to reduce their agricultural subsidies. Pakistan has reduced its fertilizer subsidies from $178 million US to $2 million US a year and Bangladesh from $56 million US to zero."

Beneficiaries of subsidies strongly resist efforts to reduce them. According to Myers, "In Washington DC, lobbyists spend $100 million US a month to support special interests, top of the list being subsidies." Once the public becomes aware of these subsidies, and how much they cost in taxes, pressure will increase to reduce them.

In British Columbia, the government's economic policy has focused primarily on protecting the primary resource industries: forestry, mining, and fishing. However, all of these industries together directly employ less than seven percent of the total provincial labor force, and employment in these industries has been declining for years.

Fishing in British Columbia

The commercial fish catch in BC was worth $71.6 million in 1998. The annual budget for the west coast activities of Fisheries and Oceans Canada (DFO) is approximately $200 million, or roughly three times the value of the commercial fishery. In BC, revenue from sports fishing totaled $485 million in 1997, but it was probably significantly less in 1998 due to DFO's zero retention on Coho salmon announced in May of that year. Sports fishing generates about 5.6 times as much money as the commercial fishery but represents five percent of the total catch. Fishing by First Nations constitutes another five percent. Commercial fishers catch the rest.

Combined, commercial and sports fishing provided approximately 13,000 seasonal jobs in 1997, a decline of about 6,000 jobs since the early 1990s. (BC's Job Protection Commissioner, 1998). People who live in BC's smaller coastal communities held most of the jobs. This decline in employment has been devastating to the prospects for community-based fishing and for co-management of fish by communities and government. [By way of comparison, sales of outdoor equipment and clothing by Mountain Equipment Coop based in Vancouver ($120 million) and Valhalla Pure in Vernon, BC ($50 million) are 2.4 times the value of the commercial fish catch, and growing rapidly.]

The BC fishing fleet has declined to approximately 2,500 boats from about 7,500 boats 50 years ago. About 350 of these boats are the larger seiners which catch 45 to 50 percent of the salmon. A single individual billionaire, Jim Pattison, now owns or controls most of these larger boats. Pattison's Canadian Fishing Company was one of the biggest on the coast even before it bought out Weston Foods' BC Packers last year. A recent report indicates that "DFO has diverted the resource into the hands of a venture capitalist who is busy relocating his interests to Calgary" (Glavin and Edwards 1999). This report argues strongly for "reduced corporate concentration and reassertion of public title over a public resource." The report also advocates "management by regional boards that would develop policy publicly, using local and traditional knowledge and giving communities a strong economic stake in protecting stream habitat on which all fish depend."

Fisheries and Oceans continues to resist the use of fish traps and nets in rivers although, from an ecosystem management point of view, these methods of salmon harvesting are better ways of managing individual runs and are also more economically viable.

Forestry Trends in BC and the United States

The current BC forest tenure system is functionally and structurally similar to the system that created the British East India Company in 1600 and the Hudson's Bay Company in 1670. Although clear, straight-grained lumber cut from old-growth forests has become an extremely valuable and globally scarce resource, the forest industry in BC treats it as though there were an unlimited supply. Because virtually all of BC's old-growth timber has been allocated to the large timber companies, there is little opportunity for smaller companies without timber tenure to add significant value to this resource.

The world's forests are being converted from natural ecosystems to plantations at an alarming rate. These forests include approximately 10,000 square kilometers of Canadian forests which are cleared each year (May 1998). More than ten percent of Canada's productive forest land has been so devastated by clearcutting that it can no longer produce any merchantable timber. Only 2.5 percent of Canada's forest land is protected from logging, despite the fact that in 1991, the Canadian House of Commons unanimously endorsed the idea of increasing protected parks and wilderness areas to 12 percent of all bioregions, including forested land.

Public values and priorities regarding the use of our forests are rapidly changing. Polls have indicated that Canadians place more importance on the wilderness values of our forests than they do on logging, and 80 percent disapprove of clearcutting as the dominant form of logging (Angus Reid 1989). Nearly half (46 percent in BC) would like to see an end to all logging of our remaining old-growth forests (Decima Research 1990).

A study by the US Forest Service concluded that over the next 50 years, remaining old-growth forests in the US will produce nine times as much in tourism and recreation revenues as they would in timber sales (US Forest Service 1989). From 1992 to 1997, according to the conservative US General Accounting Office figures, Americans paid $2 billion US to have their forests logged. And that doesn't take into account the effect of logging on local tourist economies. Recreation (including hunting and fishing) in US National Forests currently contributes nearly $40 US to the US economy for each dollar generated by logging and creates 30 times as many jobs. Today, logging generates only two percent of the revenues of the US National Forests. Nearly all revenue from these public forests (88 percent) now comes from recreation. The Sierra Club in the US is actively campaigning to end logging in the National Forests. The Forest Service's own recent poll revealed that 59 percent of Americans who expressed an opinion oppose timber sales and other commodity production in the US National Forests (*Sierra Magazine* July-August 1999). Representatives Cynthia McKinney and Jim Leach have coauthored the bipartisan National Forest Protection and Restoration Act, which would eliminate commercial logging on federal public lands, promote restoration, and help communities that receive logging revenue to develop a more diverse and stable economy.

Society needs wood products. But driven by industrial growth, society wastes a great deal of the wood fiber harvested and has bypassed, blocked, or ignored more environmentally benign sources of fiber for paper and many building products largely because of the massive public subsidies of the wood industry. An example of this is the suppression of hemp, which is a superior fiber for many wood and paper products and produces four to seven times the amount of fiber per year than trees. Another example is the pathetic lack of support for innovation in recycling.

The demand for ecologically sustainable forest practices is growing rapidly around the world. Greenpeace, the Sierra Club, the Rainforest Action Network, and other leading environmental organizations have been actively promoting the concept of certified wood products, and some groups have called for the boycott of forest products which are made from wood cut from old-growth forests or produced from unsustainable forest practices. The success of this campaign has convinced some companies to seek certification of their products and to change the way they log. According to BC Forest Alliance president Tom Tevlin, "The fact of the matter is that customers are beginning to ask for proof of sustainable management and that needs to be listened to."

A group of 27 companies, including Dell Computer Corp., Kinko's Ltd., Levi Strauss and Co., Minnesota Mining and Manufacturing Co., International Business Machines Corp., Nike Inc., Starbucks Coffee Co., and Hallmark Cards Inc. said last December that they would no longer use products from the BC coast. Together, these companies spend about $2 billion (US) on wood and paper products. (*Financial Post* August 27, 1999)

Home Depot sells wood products at its 856 stores in the United States, Canada, Chile, and Puerto Rico. Home Depot is the largest retailer of wood products in the world with nearly ten percent of total sales. In June 1999, Greenpeace launched a campaign to boycott US-based Home Depot's Canadian stores, accusing the firm of having a hand in the "destruction of the world's remaining ancient forests" (*Province*, June 6, 1999). Partly in response to the public campaign against the company, Annette Verschuren, president of Home Depot Canada, told 400 forest industry executives at a conference in Vancouver that "We believe third-party certification is essential for credibility in the market." She announced that the firm has joined the Certified Forest Products Council (CFPC), a nonprofit organization that advocates buying forest products that have been evaluated for environmental and social values at every stage, from the forest to the customer.

In August 1999, Home Depot said it will no longer sell wood products cut from endangered forests, including British Columbia's coastal rainforest (Financial Post, August 27, 1999). In making this announcement, Arthur Blank, president of Home Depot, said the new policy will include giving preference to "certified" wood that builds in social, economic, and environmental factors in foreign wood products. "Today, the world supply of certified wood is extremely limited," he said. " We are asking our vendors to help us by dramatically increasing the supply of certified forest products."

The demand for certified wood products has grown sevenfold during 1998.

Much of that demand is for wood products approved by certifiers accredited by the Forest Stewardship Council (FSC). Although initiated by the environmental movement, the FSC currently operates with equal representation from environmental, social, and economic interests. Today, most forestry operations that are FSC-accredited could best be described as benevolent industrial forestry, including some tree farms and a substantial amount of clearcutting. Initially, the certification movement was an environmental initiative to encourage ecological sustainability in forestry practices. Ideally, future certification efforts by the FSC will focus more on the objective of certifying high-quality, ecologically responsible forestry and refuse certification of high-volume industrial forestry practices such as clearcutting.

Subsidizing the BC Forest Industry

The change in public attitudes towards industrial forestry indicates that there is little support for continuing the massive perverse subsidy of the forest industry in British Columbia. However, determining the precise amount of this subsidy and its effects is extremely difficult because of the complexities inherent in the industry, the multitude of government support programs, the lack of available key data, the unwillingness to address the topic openly, and the inherent difficulty in assigning dollar figures to environmental services. What follows is a far from perfect account of subsidies or, more accurately, "the direct and indirect public costs of the BC forest industry."

For purposes of this discussion, a subsidy involves both offsetting industry costs with money derived from tax revenue (or other nonmonetary benefits to the industry) and not charging industry for many environmental costs that industry creates because of its negative effect on the land. In reality, however, subsidies are not simple. Some subsidies create public benefits such as jobs or environmental protection. However, a significant amount of subsidies contributes directly to corporate profits. Some subsidies exceed the amount the industry pays to workers. Some subsidies create conflicts of interest because they make governments into business owners as well as regulators. Most subsidies fall somewhere in the middle between support for public and private interests.

The central point here is that subsidies to the BC forest industry are higher than they would need to be if their only purpose was to create public benefits. The present size of the subsidy creates an unlevel playing field and gives the forest industry an unfair advantage relative to other interests and sectors of the economy. It is also unfair for the industry to expect taxpayers (or the environment and other industries) to subsidize forestry practices when good practices should be part of the normal cost of doing business and be financed by revenues from timber extraction.

Figure 6 summarizes the estimated direct and indirect public costs of the BC forest industry. Included in this estimate are direct expenditures by the Canadian and BC governments and taxation benefits given to forest industry corporations. Also included are other financial transfers and benefits to the companies, such as

On average, the subsidy per forestry worker in BC is $136,000 per year.

corporate bailouts, lost stumpage, and environmental damage from logging.

The two largest components of the total amount estimated in Figure 6 are lost government revenue and environmental damages from logging. The other components are actual government expenditures and tax benefits. A large part of these direct and indirect public costs of the BC forest industry are perverse subsidies. Perverse subsidies provide neither economic nor ecological public benefits and can cause damage to the environment. It will require much more research to estimate the precise extent of perverse subsidies – and the damage they cause.

Most of the amounts listed in Figure 6 are based on a comprehensive study of the industry by economist Michael Mascall. Mascall's analysis details expenditures for the eight years 1988 to 1996 (Mascall 1997). Because of the fluctuations in the forest industry economy and changing government programs, Mascall uses the average annual expenditure for these eight years. Estimates of other subsidies are based on other research, as indicated in Figure 6 and the following discussion.

The BC forest industry receives benefits from many agencies of the Canadian government, particularly from Forestry Canada. Forestry Canada programs include the Forest Resource Development Agreement (FRDA I), through which the federal government spent $150 million in BC between 1985 and 1989. Between 1990 and 1995, the federal government spent an additional $100 million in the province through FRDA II. The forest industry constitutes one of the six branches in the Industry and Technology Development Sector of Industry Canada, which provides research and development assistance. The total amount of annual trans-

Figure 6:
Direct & Indirect
Annual Public Costs
of the BC Forest Industry
($Millions) August, 1999.

	Annual Average 1989-96*	Current Rough Estimate**	Estimated Total Subsidies
DIRECT GOVERNMENT AGENCY EXPENDITURES:			
Canadian Government:			
Forestry Canada	$80		$80
Foreign Affairs & International Trade	8		8
Industry Canada	39		39
National Research Council	2		2
Natural Science and Engineering Research Council	20		20
Energy Mines and Resources	13		13
Environment Canada	33		33
Western Economic Diversification	20		20
Total Canadian Government			**$215**
Provincial Government:			
Ministry of Forests (90% of total ministry budget) (Mascall 1997)		$558	$558
Ministry of Environment (30% of total ministry budget) (Mascall 1997)		60	60
Ministry of Employment & Investment	$18		18
Ministry of Advanced Education, Training & Technology	41		41
Ministry of Skills, Training and Labour	5		5
Ministry of Transport & Highways	20		20
Forest Renewal (two year average 1995-96) (Mascall 1997)	472		472
Ministry of Energy, Mines and Petroleum Resouces	6		6
Total Provincial Government			**$1,180**
TOTAL DIRECT GOVERNMENT AGENCY EXPENDITURES			**$1,395**
TAXATION BENEFITS:			
Preferential Rates	$210		$210
Deferred Taxes (Interest Saved)	130		130
Tax Credits	57		57
Total Taxation Benefits			**$397**
OTHER FINANCIAL TRANSFERS:			
Payments for Land Removed from License Areas		$84	$84
Bailouts of Troubled Forest Companies		287	287
Total Financial Transfers			**$371**
INDIRECT PUBLIC COSTS:			
"Stumpage Fees Foregone: (FRC, Major, Mascall, M'Gonigle)"			$5,016
Damage-Related Costs:			
Sediment-Related Off-Site Damage from Logging (adapted from Neimi 1999)		$2,950	$2,950
On-Site Degradation of Logged Areas (Utzig & Walmsley)		140	140
Quality-of-Life Damages from Logging (unknown)		-	-
Total Damage-Related Costs			**$3,090**
Total Indirect Public Costs			**$8,106**
Total Direct & Indirect Annual Public Costs of the BC Forest Industry			**$10,269**
Annual Direct & Indirect Annual Public Cost for Each of 75,238 Forest Employees			$0.136

Source of estimates indicated in the 2nd column (*) are from Mascall 1997 (based on eight-year average 1989-96).
Sources of the rough estimates in the 3rd column (**) are indicated following item descriptions in 1st column.

fers from the Canadian government to the forest industry in BC has averaged $215 million annually during the eight year period, 1986-95.

Transfers from the BC government to the forest industry include most of the cost of the provincial Ministry of Forests (MoF), which spends nearly $620 million a year to administer timber extraction and silvicultural treatments (Ministry of Forests annual reports). Although some of this cost covers services that would be necessary even without logging, most of it is attributable to logging. Services not related to logging include part or most of fire-fighting costs. They also include recreation services, which have never amounted to more than one percent of the total MoF budget. That leaves approximately 90 percent of MoF's budget which is spent on tasks related to logging.

In addition to MoF expenditures, the Ministry of Environment (MoE) spends roughly $60 million a year on forests, because MoE staff spend approximately 30 percent of their time monitoring the logging and road-building activities of the forest industry. The provincial government also spends money on the forest industry through its Forest Renewal BC program. The government created Forest Renewal BC in June 1994 to "renew the forest economy of BC, enhance the productive capacity and environmental value of forest lands, create jobs, provide training for forest workers, and strengthen communities" (BC Public Accounts, 1994-95). In 1994 and 1995, the program spent an average of $472 million in revenues from stumpage, the money the industry pays to the MoF on timber extracted. This annual figure has dropped since the mid-1990s. In total, the BC government has been spending an average of $1.180 billion a year to support the forest industry.

The forest industry has also enjoyed a number of tax benefits, including various forms of income tax relief which represent lost government revenues. These tax benefits include $210 million a year in preferential rates, $130 million a year in interest saved from deferred taxes, and $57 million a year in tax credits. In total, taxation benefits averaged $397 million a year.

Other financial transfers to the forest industry include payments from government to forest companies for land removed from their license areas. An example of this is BC's recent agreement to pay MacMillan Bloedel (MB) $83.75 million for MB's loss of harvesting rights on Vancouver Island because of the creation of new parks in the mid-1990s. No doubt other forest companies will try to make similar deals. In fact, negotiations are imminent in a dozen other situations.

Financial transfers also include bailouts of troubled forest companies. One example was the $240 million in 1997, $329 million in 1998, and $257 million in May 1999 that the BC government provided to Skeena Cellulose in Prince Rupert. The amount of capital, credit, and other funding Skeena Cellulose has received from the taxpayers of BC has totaled $826 million during the past three years. This amounts to $340,000 for each one of the company's 2,400 employees. The BC government now owns 52 percent of the company, which continues to lose money. No one knows precisely how much the company is losing, because the BC government

Loading BC logs for export.

has refused to release financial statements for 1998 and the first quarter of 1999. Skeena Cellulose's ability to function depends on its ability to continue overharvesting the vast timberlands in the company's lease. As forest industry analyst Charles Widman explains, "...the time has come when the government should level with the taxpayers in BC and tell us exactly how much the government has invested in Skeena, both in direct and contingent liabilities" (*Province* May 27, 1999). Another example is the $14 million in 1997 and an additional $21.5 million in 1998 that the government gave to Evans Forest Products in the East Kootenay region of the province. There may be other politically motivated bailouts of the forest industry that we don't know about or that are under consideration. The total that we know about amounts to $861 between 1995 and 1998 or $287 million a year.

By far the largest financial benefits the forest industry receives come from foregone stumpage fees. This refers to the difference between the price the logs would bring on the open market and the amount BC logging companies pay to the provincial government in stumpage, or cutting fees. Forestry consultant Michael Major, who worked in the industry for many years, has estimated this difference at $6 billion annually. He estimates that this concession to the BC coastal forest industry costs the public an average of $122 per cubic meter on a harvest base of 23 million cubic meters, or about $2.8 billion a year. For interior BC, he estimates this public cost at an average of $60 per cubic meter on a harvest base of 53 million cubic meters, or about $3.2 billion per year. These figures may seem high, but we know that timber sells on the Seattle log market for 85 and 200 percent more than similar timber brings on the Vancouver log market. In the interior of the province, the MoF created the Vernon log yard to sell timber on the open market, and this log yard generates at least $40 per cubic meter more than the government receives from the large forest tenure holders in the area. The timber sold at the Vernon log yard is sorted and displayed for purchasers, and a significant amount has been harvested with more costly and ecologically sound methods.

Several economists have developed similar estimates of foregone stumpage. The Forest Resource Commission estimated foregone stumpage at between $1.773 and $5.319 billion (as quoted in Gale, Gale and Green 1999). Economist Michael Mascall has estimated the overall average value of foregone stumpage fees could be as much as $6 billion per year (Mascall and Campbell 1997). In 1997, Mascall cited a smaller amount, using a more conservative approach based on the calculations of the US Department of Commerce in their remand study. Using the US figures, Mascall estimated that foregone stumpage ranged between $1.95 and $2.305 billion. However, in my discussions with him during August 1999, he told me that he believed his higher $6 billion estimate is more accurate. Political economist Michael M'Gonigle came up with estimates ranging between $3.546 and $5.319 billion (M'Gonigle and Parfitt 1994). The average of the four estimates ranges between $4.351 and 5.681 billion. For purposes of this discussion, I have chosen to use a mid-range value of $5.016 billion for foregone stumpage.[4]

Environmental damages to the ecology of the land base and to our quality of life present the most difficult challenge in estimating indirect public costs of the BC forest industry. These costs include logging-related damage to community watersheds, fish-bearing watersheds, viewscapes, and the potential for tourism and recreation. In the United States, the value of these resources have often exceeded the value of logging. Grant and Wolff determined that clearcutting alone can generate an additional one ton of runoff per acre in the US, and clearcutting plus logging roads can generate 3.5 tons per acre per year for about 25 years. These numbers indicate that the off-site spill-over costs that logging imposes on others because of sediment-related damage alone can be more than $250 per acre. The Northwest Forest Plan removed a total of 18.8 million acres from logging. Estimates indicate that this protected forest land reduced potential sediment-related costs by $4.7 billion (Grant and Wolff as quoted by Niemi and Johnston 1999). Ministry of Forests figures indicate that 4,779,243 hectares were logged in

---

4: I rejected a fifth estimate that was based on a Ricardian rent approach that subtracts harvesting and capital costs from the value of wood shipments (B. Grafton, Lynch, and Nelson 1998, as quoted in Gale, Gale and Green 1999). The BC Ministry of Forests also uses the Ricardian approach in calculating stumpage. The huge discrepancy between the Ricardian estimate and the four market-value estimates suggests that the Ministry of Forests has substantially undervalued wood products and/or overestimated costs in its determination of stumpage. These estimates of foregone stumpage do not include the amount of stumpage the government actually collected ($1.773 billion in 1997). Nor do they include production costs. In a market-based approach to estimating foregone stumpage, the amount buyers are willing to pay in the open marketplace includes production costs, stumpage paid, and profits.

BC during the 25 years 1971-1995, an average of 191,173 hectares per year. Logging and logging roads have caused many damaging landslides and debris torrents in BC. Most of them cause significant damage to adjacent private and public property, not to mention fish habitat. (See photos of Memphis Creek clearcut and highway washout on page 36) Forest ecologist Herb Hammond estimates that sediment-related damages could amount to as much as $1,000 per acre ($2,500 per hectare) per year over periods of up to 100 years. Multiplying the US figure of $250 per acre ($617 per hectare) per year times 25 years times the average 191,173 hectares logged per year amounts to $2.95 billion per year. Multiplying by 25 years accounts for the amount of land which remains susceptible to damage. Hammond's figures suggest that these costs could be several times this amount. The figure of $2.95 billion in Figure 6 is therefore a conservative estimate, and it is probably much less than it would cost to stop off-site damages from logging across the whole provincial forest base.

One of many costs included in the above estimate of sediment-related damage from logging is damage to salmon habitat. Greenpeace recently released a report that states it would cost $4 billion to restore BC's salmon habitat, citing a 1997 study by Ministry of Environment biologists. This study concluded that up to 20,000 kilometers of streams have a "potential need of 20 to 40 years of slope and stream rehabilitation," with an estimated cost of $50 to $100 million per year. The report also claims that the BC Forest Practice Code has proved "inadequate in correcting...destructive practices." (Province August 19, 1999) Sediment-related damage from logging also causes damages to private property. A recent issue of *McLean's Magazine* indicated that insurance claims from manmade disasters have increased 1,600 percent. Insurance companies are predicting substantial increases in premiums.

Logging also causes damages to the logged area. These on-site damages are in addition to off-site damages. Two experienced soils scientists developed a comprehensive estimate of forest degradation in logged areas in BC over the ten-year period 1976 to 1986 (Utzig and Walmsley 1988). They documented degradation of 403,551 ha or 21.6 percent of logged areas. 1.87 million hectares were logged during this ten-year period, or roughly 190,000 hectares per year. Utzig and Walmsley estimated that the cost of rehabilitating these degraded sites ranged between $500 and $5,000 per hectare. The scientists estimated that preventing the damage by using alternative harvesting systems would cost between $250 and $1,800 per hectare and between zero and $200 per hectare for improving pre-harvest planning. Using a conservative average of $1,000 per hectare, the cost of rehabilitation and/or prevention would be $40 million per year plus the cost of rehabilitating areas which were logged in the past. It would cost $100 million per year over the next 20 years to rehabilitate the degraded sites logged during the past 50 years. This $100 million per year plus $40 million for current logging would total $140 million per year over the next 20 years. The estimate of the total losses to the provincial economy as a result of forestry practices is approximately $126 million per year. This is over three times the rehabilitation/prevention costs of $40 million per year (Utzig and Walmsley 1988). However, to be on the conservative side, Figure 6 uses the lower number.

The last, but far from the least important public cost is logging's effect on our quality of life. As Thomas Power has suggested (Power 1988,1996), clean air and water, abundant wildlife populations, natural forested areas, and other qualities have become the primary attractions when people are choosing a place to live in the western United States. A study of the Pacific northwest (Niemi 1999) identified the value of quality of life as of major importance to a community's economic vitality. Although it is difficult to estimate the dollar value of maintaining quality of life in the US or Canada, it is a significant issue. Research is urgently needed to determine these costs. A lack of accurate information made it impossible to include an estimate for the depreciation of quality of life in Figure 6. Nevertheless, in my opinion, which is based on anecdotal assessments, I estimate that these costs could be as much as $6,000 per taxpayer or about $16 billion a year in BC. This rough estimate includes the value of clean water and air, minimal noise pollution, the value of viewscapes, proximity to pristine wilderness and parks, soil conservation, low levels of toxins, ecosystem stability (presence of animals and protection of biodiversity), good health, a good future for our children, low crime rates, an ecologically sustainable economy, community stability (e.g., continuity of friendships), and fewer auto accidents. My estimate is based on how much people would be willing to pay to maintain a high quality of life or the difference between a high quality of life and a low quality of life. Although I recognize the speculative nature of this calculation, I estimate that logging-related activities could account for approximately 25 percent of this amount, or about $4 billion a year.

The taxpayers of BC are receiving artificially low rent for the use of public forests. The rent consists of relatively low stumpage fees and other minimal fees that industry pays for the use of publicly owned forests. Because these returns are less than the public costs incurred, the forest industry has received a sustained and very substantial net subsidy. Since the US forest industry is also subsidized, the numbers in Figure 6 further underestimate the potential market value of BC logs. According to one source (Rasker, Gorte, and Alkire 1997), US taxpayers are subsidizing National Forest timber harvesting at the rate of about $300 million (US) a year, or about $1,000 (US) for every job in the primary wood-processing industries.

The estimated cost of the forest industry to the public[5] excludes items such as the cost of litigation and maintaining public order when there is public opposition to logging operations. These costs can be substantial, as indicated by the $1.5

5: Price Waterhouse (one of the forest industry's economic consultants) and the BC government often characterize corporate and personal income taxes paid by the forest industry as benefits to the public. Price Waterhouse uses these taxes to offset the cost of services that the industry receives from governments. However, this practice makes no logical sense because everyone living in Canada and BC is required to pay income taxes: school teachers, doctors, lawyers, and farmers, as well as forestry workers. Income and sales taxes are used primarily to finance services such as education and health care, and to pay interest on government debt.

million already spent in connection with the controversial Perry Ridge area in the Slocan Valley of BC (Gale, Gale, and Green 1999). The cost of this litigation, plus other money the government is spending on road construction, planning processes, and administration, exceeds the amount of return the government can expect from logging this relatively small area. (The area contains only 2,400 hectares of stable and moderately stable terrain suitable for timber management.) The figures in Figure 6 also exclude the cost of logging-related damages to land transferred to First Nations under land claim settlements. These costs can be significant. Price Waterhouse's 1995 report for the Nisga'a Tribal Council assessed restoration costs at $262 million. Nor do the figures include the cost of depreciating natural capital. Logging in BC has gone way beyond the rate that would be ecologically sustainable. Achieving a sustainable rate of logging would require a minimum province-wide 60 to 70 percent reduction of the present allowable annual cut. Revenue from logging that is not ecologically sustainable depletes natural resources and cannot be considered as income. Other costs of logging should include neglect of alternative economic uses such as ecotourism, botanical forest products, and recreation user fees (Gale, Gale, and Green, 1999). Again due to lack of available information, Figure 6 does not include these costs.

Because no one knows the real costs of many of the consequences of logging, the total picture of direct and indirect public costs of the BC forest industry is incomplete, but it is undoubtedly more than the $10.269 billion a year indicated in Figure 6. This staggering amount works out to approximately $136,000 a year for each of BC's 75,238 forest industry employees. According to Statistics Canada, in 1997 there were 2.658 million tax filers in BC. During this year, the annual public costs of the forest industry averaged nearly $3,863 a year for every BC taxpayer. Taxpayers paid only part of this directly; the rest was potential revenue that the government never collected, plus damages to the environment. This $10.269 billion figure is a rough and incomplete estimate and we have yet to discover the extent of perverse subsidies.

Of course, many people will adamantly dispute these figures. But even the more conservative estimates of the overall public costs of the BC forest industry range between $1.66 and $4.23 billion a year (Gale, Gale, and Green, 1999). Using the median conservative estimate of $2.93 billion, the annual public cost per forestry worker would be $38,943 and $1,102 per taxpayer. By any accounts, these numbers are huge.

Keeping up this level of subsidy for the BC forest industry is impoverishing BC's political, environmental, economic, and social infrastructure. It discourages ingenuity and entrepreneurial activity and retards the potential growth in market value of BC's forest products. It has also driven taxes up to the point where some of the province's most promising high technology companies are having difficulty keeping their employees. Some companies are moving their operations to Alberta and the US. Perhaps the growth of free trade, which in principle prohibits subsidies, will eliminate some of the perverse subsidies for the BC forest industry. But this is doubtful in the current climate of the increasing globalization of economic activity because globalization tends to serve the interests of larger transnational corporations over those of smaller community-based entrepreneurs.

The BC government needs to take bold and immediate action to reduce and eventually eliminate perverse subsidies for the forest industry. Some of the money saved could be used to help laid-off forestry workers during the necessary transition, to improve logging practices, and to increase the value of BC's forest products. Companies that resist these changes could lose their forest tenures. These tenures could be divided into smaller units and allocated to communities and community-based companies that have been asking for more control over forestry decisions. The overall economy will also benefit from reducing perverse subsidies. The BC government has no rational reason to delay acting on this crucially important issue.

Chapter 16

THE GREEN ECONOMY: MAKING IT HAPPEN

This chapter suggests several ways of developing a green economy – investing more in the parks system, changing the tax structure, and a system for evaluating and supporting community-based economic development projects.

Improving the Parks System – A Good Investment

The economic benefits from establishing nationally significant protected areas like the Stikine and the Kitlope, can be significant. The success of Gwaii Haanas/South Moresby National Park Reserve which was established in 1987 illustrates the kind of returns that are possible. Although it is unlikely that a provincial park could generate the same scale of revenues as Gwaii Haanas, the principle is the same: economic benefits from the new national park have exceeded the economic benefits from the forest industry before the park was established. And timber values per hectare within Gwaii Haanas are many times higher than timber values in the Stikine and similar park areas.

According to one study (Broadhead 1995), the economic effects of Gwaii Haanas have included an average of $6.5 million per year in direct spending in the local economy on Haida Gwaii. In the long term, annual spending will amount to over $10 million.

The park has created 35 Parks Canada job positions, 13 of which are Haida. Planning, management, and operations in Gwaii Haanas provide another 15 person-years of employment distributed among 50 people. This work includes the Haida Gwaii Watchman Program, which provides on-site guardian services for significant sites within Gwaii Haanas.

Tourists who come to Haida Gwaii specifically to visit Gwaii Haanas spent more than $2 million per year during the 1990-92 seasons. These visitors created 16 person-years of direct employment. This compares to a total of $3.1 million per year that employees earned from logging in the Gwaii Haanas portion of TFL 24, and much of this money left the local economy with workers who were off-island residents. Sandspit, Skidegate, and Queen Charlotte City have all registered increases in population and the number of residents in the labor force.

The most unexpected outcome of the South Moresby Agreement has been the development of sustainability at the community level. Local planning and decision-making processes have challenged island communities and cultures to work together to overcome differences that have often divided them in the past.

One consultant's report (Coopers and Lybrand Consulting 1996) shows that the parks system in BC has generated economic activity that sustains about 9,500 direct and indirect jobs and contributes $420 million to the provincial gross domestic product (GDP). For each dollar the BC government spends on parks, British Columbians see a return of about nine dollars in spending by visitors. This includes money for food and accommodation, guided tours, and supplies and equipment. In addition, people who use the parks get significant benefits from recreation activities beyond what they buy. Consumer surplus is the difference between what people would be willing to pay for goods or services and what they actually have to pay. For 1994, Coopers and Lybrand estimated these nonmarket benefits (consumer surplus) at approximately $760 million, net of the cost of operating the park system.

The Coopers and Lybrand study also estimated the value of new parks added between 1991 and October 1995. With the addition of these parks (but not other parks which have been added since October 1995), visitor spending should top $600 million by 2002 and support 14,000 jobs. Consumer surplus will probably reach $1.2 billion by 2002. In 1994, the provincial government spent $35.3 million on the park system and received $42 million in tax revenue. The Coopers and Lybrand study projected government expenditures of $55 million for 2002 (with the parks added before October 1995) and tax revenues of $60 million. The consultants noted that "for a system that has conservation as a primary objective, the financial flows of revenue and expense to the provincial account are roughly in balance."

The potential return on investment in parks suggests that it would make good ecological and economic sense for the provincial government to allocate more funding to increasing and developing BC's system of provincial parks. These improvements could include more interpretive services, improvements to park infrastructure (especially trails), increasing the number of back-country rangers, and completing management plans for parks. Additional funding could also help to increase the participation of First Nations in establishing, managing and patrolling provincial parks.

Although the provincial park system has nearly doubled in size over the past decade, the provincial government has continued to cut the funding for BC Parks. According to reliable sources within BC Parks, to do the necessary work of managing the 11 percent of BC lands that are protected in parks, the budget for BC Parks should be at least triple the present allocation of $35 million. BC's Park Legacy Project (Legacy Panel 1998) has recommended doubling the budget for parks, but this will not be enough because the size of the park system has doubled and the demands of the public and the growing tourism industry for services have increased substantially at the same time that the budget has been reduced.

Old growth spruce tree, South Moresby National Park Reserve.

Shifting Taxes in Favor of the Environment

Fritjof Capra advocates an ecological tax reform that would tax unsustainable resource use and reward ecologically sound practices, including ecologically sustainable energy use, forestry, and fishing. Northwest Environment Watch, an environmental advocacy group based in Seattle, has produced a report that outlines how the tax system in the Pacific northwest could be changed to improve the environment and reduce income and sales taxes (Durning and Bauman 1998). The authors of this report focus on the states of Washington, Oregon, parts of Alaska, Idaho, Montana, and California, plus the part of British Columbia that drains into the Pacific Ocean.

According to economists, an ideal tax system would charge polluters for the costs they impose on others. These costs include environmental damage, impact on health, and economic losses. Estimates of human and environmental costs of pollution indicate that optimal pollution tax rates are many times higher than the current penalties. For example, the penalty for emitting a ton of sulphur dioxide is about $50 in most regions of the northwest, but the actual costs, including crop losses, building corrosion, impaired visibility, and respiratory illnesses, may be $5,000 or more. Northwest Environment Watch estimates that, had pollution taxes been in place in 1995, they would have raised $3.1 billion in the northwest and achieved a 15 percent reduction in emissions (Durning and Bauman 1998).

While "clean" companies would benefit, "dirty" companies would pay for the pollution they cause. One analysis of the impact of water pollution in Washington State found that more than half of pollution taxes would be levied against polluters in one industry: pulp and paper manufacturing. The BC government was the first in the world to establish a deadline – the year 2002 – for the elimination of dioxins and other deadly byproducts of chlorine bleaching (Durning and Bauman 1998).

Northwest Environmental Watch advocates several new taxes on carbon production, pollution, traffic, urban sprawl, and resource consumption. Revenues generated from these new taxes could be used to reduce income and sales taxes. Most importantly, these new taxes would make a major contribution towards resolving the growing problem of climate change.

Carbon fuels could be taxed in proportion to the carbon dioxide they emit. Other greenhouse gases could also be taxed. These taxes would raise the prices of gasoline, electricity produced from coal, and other forms of energy that contribute to climate change. During and Bauman calculate that a tax of $100 per ton of carbon dioxide, with parallel rates on other greenhouse gases, could have raised $5.8 billion in the northwest in 1994 and could have reduced emissions by 15 percent. These new taxes could offset more than one-fourth of all payroll taxes collected in the region and save the typical working household $852 a year. A tax of this magnitude would add eight cents to the price of a gallon of gasoline in the US and three cents per liter in Canada. It would increase the wholesale price of natural gas by 14 percent and raise the price of coal by 49 percent (Durning and Bauman 1998).

Emissions of greenhouse gases are now 16 percent above 1990 levels in BC, mostly due to poor land-use and transportation decisions in the lower mainland. Despite the creation of a multistakeholder Greenhouse Gas Forum, the BC government has not developed an aggressive strategy to reduce greenhouse gases. Moreover, the BC government has announced a significant increase in oil and gas production in the province's northeast boreal region. This has implications for acid rain and air quality as well as for climate change. BC Hydro is also increasing its greenhouse gas emissions through investments in gas-fired co-generation facilities (May 1998). BC Hydro has failed to implement most of the recommendations in its study of energy conservation opportunities. Instead of helping to reduce global warming, the British Columbia and Canadian governments are making the situation worse.

Pollution taxes would be aimed at reducing the toxic chemicals and other dangerous substances from manufacturing processes and runoffs of manure and other fertilizers from farms. The effects of toxic chemicals are difficult to prove. However, we know that sperm counts have fallen 50 percent since World War II, and cancer now strikes more than one in three and kills about one in four North Americans (Durning and Bauman 1998).

Regulations are sometimes the best way to control the most dangerous chemicals, but taxes can also discourage the use of dangerous substances. Northwest Environment Watch cites two examples. In the Netherlands, a hefty charge for dumping lead, mercury, and other heavy metals into rivers is the main reason that water pollution levels dropped more than 90 percent between 1975 and 1995. As part of the phase-out of ozone-depleting chlorofluorocarbons (CFCs) in the early 1990s, the US government imposed taxes that raised CFC prices as much as eleven-fold, spurring innovations that quickly produced low-cost alternatives (Durning and Bauman 1998).

Sewer systems could be vastly improved in municipalities like Vancouver, BC – where the Annacis Island plant regularly shows up on BC's list of the province's worst polluters – and Victoria, BC, which dumps most of its sewage untreated into the Strait of Juan de Fuca.

The Sierra Legal Defense Fund (SLDF) has laid charges against the Capital Regional District (CRD) on behalf of the CAW-United Fishermen and Allied Workers Union Local 24. The union members are concerned about the impact of the sewage on fish and shellfish populations. Over 40 square kilometers of the ocean off Victoria have been closed to shellfish harvesting as a result of contamination by CRD sewage. More than 500,000 square meters of the sea floor near the sewage outflow pipe are covered in a decomposing pile of human waste, contaminated with heavy metals and toxic organic chemicals. Since 1986, both the provincial and federal governments have repeatedly advised the CRD to upgrade its sewage treatment system, but the CRD has failed to comply. SLDF lawyers have brought six prosecutions before the BC courts, but the government has taken over all six cases, and the court subsequently stayed the proceedings (SLDF 1999). Seattle dumped 2.2 billion gallons of raw sewage into the waters of Puget Sound in 1996. Again, these continuing environmental subsidies undermine the growth potential for innovative businesses such as Ballard and Hydroxyl (see Chapter 13).

Instead of allowing such discharges, pollution taxes would give coal-burning power plants, like the one in Centralia, Washington, whose sulphur emissions are estimated to kill more than 19 people each year, an economic incentive to reduce harmful emissions while increasing the demand for other forms of energy. (Durning and Bauman 1998).

Pollution taxes would encourage manufacturers and cities to stop investing in and dumping vast quantities of chemicals and sewage and to start investing in the innovations that offer low-cost pollution solutions. A properly designed pollution tax would make prices tell the truth about the environmental damage from manufacturing and waste management processes.

The best long-term strategy for encouraging the development and purchase of cleaner vehicles would be to change the tax rates on new cars (Puget Sound Regional Council 1995). The worst polluting vehicles would pay much higher taxes than cleaner vehicles. Traffic taxes in crowded metropolitan areas would encourage more people to use public transit and provide funding for new subway and bus systems. It has been predicted that even if the Seattle area raises $1 billion extra each year to spend on mass transit and other transportation improvements, afternoon gridlock will spread to almost half the freeway network in the central

Figure 7: Tax Shift Scenario

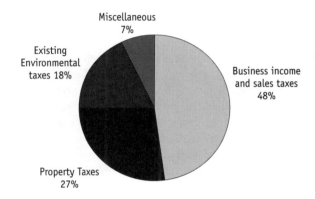

ACTUAL EXISTING

Miscellaneous
7%

Existing
Environmental
taxes 18%

Business income
and sales taxes
48%

Property Taxes
27%

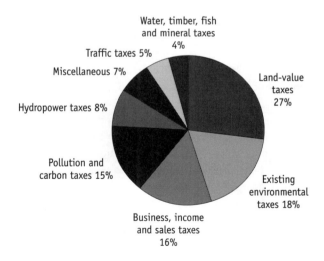

TAX SHIFT SCENARIO

Water, timber, fish
and mineral taxes
4%

Traffic taxes 5%

Miscellaneous 7%

Hydropower taxes 8%

Pollution and
carbon taxes 15%

Land-value
taxes
27%

Existing
environmental
taxes 18%

Business, income
and sales taxes
16%

Source: *Tax Shift*, Alan Durning and Yoram Bauman,
Northwest Environmental Watch, 1998

Puget Sound region by the year 2020. The time residents spend stuck in traffic will grow threefold over 1995 levels, and average highway speeds will fall to 21 miles per hour. In Vancouver, BC, rush hours will tie up 60 percent more vehicles in 2021 than in 1992 (GVRD 1993).

Figure 7 illustrates the Northwest Environment Watch tax-shift scenario (Durning and Bauman 1998). In this scenario, business, income, and sales taxes would be reduced from 48 percent to 16 percent of the total tax burden. New taxes on pollution and carbon (15 percent), traffic (five percent), hydropower (eight percent), and water, timber, fish and minerals (four percent) would make up the difference.

Setting Priorities for Government Support of Community-Based Projects

Political processes such as lobbying by industry, labor unions, other special interest groups, and individuals with political influence determine the degree of government support for economic development projects. The economic development priorities of governments have usually had little relationship to the need for community-based economic development, important and often critical environmental issues, or even the economic feasibility of development proposals.

The BC and Canadian governments have supported the resource extraction industries, but they have provided little support for the fastest growing segments of the economy. These include the high-tech sector, tourism, and film making. One of the most promising companies in the province is Ballard Power. Government assistance to Ballard Power represents a small percentage of the subsidies available to the leading forestry companies, each of which is a much smaller company than Ballard.

Governments need criteria for evaluating economic development options. Economies will benefit from rational evaluation of economic development proposals. Governments need to eliminate perverse subsidies and replace them with government assistance to the most promising economic sectors. This transition strategy would expand employment opportunities, reduce detrimental effects on the environment, and enhance opportunities for small, community-based businesses. This strategy has worked in Oregon and Washington, and it can also be successful in British Columbia.

Government approval and/or funding for economic development projects could depend on a process of rational evaluation that uses a weighted point system, with positive points for projects that demonstrate good ecological economics and negative points for projects that are detrimental to the environment and/or impose costs on others.

One element in the evaluation would be the degree of local participation and investment in the project. The points system could reflect the percentage of local ownership of economic development projects. The larger the percentage of local ownership, the more positive points. The number of local persons (employees, working directors, and others) working on the project would be a second factor in the evaluation. The absolute number of local workers could be a factor and also the number of local workers relative to the amount of capital invested and/or the amount of land being used. This measure reflects the labor intensity of the project: the higher the intensity or the more jobs per dollar invested or land used, the more points the project would receive. Worker ownership could earn bonus points.

A third element would be whether or not there is support of the project by local and regional governments, local members of provincial or state and federal legislative assemblies, and affected First Nations. Letters of support from local municipal councils and band councils should earn positive points, especially when the support of these representatives is consistent with established economic development policies for the area. Municipal and regional district officials who administer economic development policy on behalf of elected boards could submit letters to the hearing examiner or government approving authority for projects that comply with established policies.

The desirability of the proposed land use relative to existing and proposed or planned public and industrial uses should be another factor in the evaluation. It will not be easy to evaluate this factor when existing industrial users (e.g., logging companies) and existing public users (e.g., snowmobile clubs) make competing claims. These conflicts are extremely difficult to resolve at the project evaluation stage. It would be more effective to resolve conflicts between different land uses in advance of development proposals through comprehensive land-use planning processes that encompass local and/or regional levels. Comprehensive land-use planning processes could resolve these conflicts by assigning incompatible land uses to different areas. It is also important to allow enough time in the evaluation process so that government agencies and the public can react to proposed projects, but not so much time that competing users will have a chance to increase their use of the area during the evaluation process. Projects that conflict with other uses would get negative points. Projects that fit well with other uses would get positive points. Projects that are more sustainable and more acceptable to the local community than existing or other uses could also earn positive points.

Another criterion would be the degree of mechanized use and the intensity of land use. Projects that limit the use of mechanized transportation (e.g., ski touring and hiking) would have priority over highly mechanized uses (e.g., helicopter skiing, snowmobiling, and snowcat skiing). Projects that require lesser amounts of land per user day (e.g., ski touring and hiking) would have priority over uses that require large amounts of territory (e.g., helicopter skiing and helicopter-access hiking). The rationale for establishing these priorities is based on the concept of generating optimum benefits from available resources with minimum environmental impact on the resources. A ski-touring project would earn more points than a helicopter-skiing project because it generates less impact on the environment and uses less land per user day.

The amount of value added in local communities, the region, and the province would influence the evaluation. Value-added within the community would be worth more points, with lesser points for value-added in the surrounding region, province, or state. The points could have a direct relationship to the percentage of value-added (e.g., furniture) relative to the value of raw materials used (e.g., timber).

The evaluation would take into account the degree to which the proposed use of natural resources is ecologically sustainable. A proposal would get positive points for compliance with ecosystem-based plans such as the one developed for the Slocan Valley. The evaluation could estimate the project's effects on biological and cultural diversity, but the results would depend on the amount of scientific evidence available and the ability of the developer to finance this work. Ecosystem-based plans are a logical responsibility of government because these plans are most effective when they are prepared on a regional or watershed scale and because plan policies should reflect the long-term public interest. Projects with the least ecological impacts would get positive points; projects that require modifications to the natural ecology would get negative points.

The evaluation would assign points for other ecological values of the project, such as energy self-sufficiency or the amount of pollution the project will create. Air, water, and noise pollution and combustion of fossil fuels would earn negative points; nonpolluting, nonconsumptive sources of energy (e.g., small hydroelectric or wind-driven power plants) would earn positive points.

Prospects for sustainable economic benefits would be an important criterion (especially for local communities and local entrepreneurs). Economic sustainability depends upon ecological sustainability and market demand for the product. Ecological sustainability is difficult to evaluate because it is necessary to compare proposed land uses to alternative uses of the land, and forecasting market demand depends on accurate estimation and projection of the long-term supply and demand for the product. Nevertheless, projects that are ecologically sustainable and/or have strong market demand could earn positive points. Projects that benefit local communities and create opportunities for local entrepreneurs could get bonus points. Projects that require substantial proportions of imported labor and capital or require temporary work camps would earn negative points.

Involving First Nations would be part of the evaluation. When projects are located within the traditional land of First Nations, projects could earn bonus points if they involve First Nations as partners and/or employ First Nations people in the construction and operation of the project.

Chapter 17

THE ACT OF BALANCE: INTEGRATING PROFITS WITH PEOPLE AND PLACE

The challenges this book presents require decisive changes in the way we manage our public affairs. One of the biggest challenges is to recognize and support more desirable projects and to oppose the undesirable ones. As Fritjof Capra puts it, this will require everyone to think and act in an ecologically literate manner. Identifying projects that are acceptable in terms of environmental impacts, social acceptability, and economic viability is not easy because these issues almost always require compromise. Making tradeoffs requires cooperation among competing and often opposing segments of communities. Interest groups have not been particularly successful in working together on this. In the absence of local or regional land-use and economic planning, major land-use and economic decision making within the province of BC usually defaults to the provincial level, where it is difficult to get agreement on what is in the best interest of communities.

In BC, the provincial government has delegated land-use planning to regional processes such as those orchestrated by the Commission on Resources and Environment (CORE) and Land and Resource Management Plans (LRMPs). These planning processes have attempted to involve multistakeholder participation. In some instances the process has been relatively successful in identifying plans and polices that are acceptable to the representatives sitting at the CORE and LRMP tables. But too often, larger corporate interests, backed by their employees and employees' unions, and with strong support from the provincial government, have dominated and/or have overruled the decisions developed through these planning processes. Often the companies and government agencies have fanned the workers' fear of losing their jobs. When this happens, the provincial government has tended to ignore ecological and economic principles, and instead has usually adopted and approved plans that do not satisfy the majority of local and regional populations. Socioeconomic considerations have all too often been expressed in terms of the needs of the employees and shareholders of large corporations. Important community-based needs, such as the fostering of small business opportunities and achieving and maintaining community ownership of businesses, have been ignored and/or rejected.

The following package of proposals could help improve the way society balances economic viability with social appropriateness and the ecological bottom line.

Foster Local Planning

The challenge for communities is to keep planning as local as possible with the focus on community-based economic development and ecosystem-based comprehensive planning. Higher-level governments could support community-based decision making and recommendations. One example is the 75 percent local support for the locally produced, ecosystem-based forest management plan in the Slocan Valley (See Chapter 4). We need community and provincial support for projects that best meet the criteria outlined in the previous chapter. If this support is not forthcoming, communities are disempowered and become more susceptible to domination by larger companies, transnational corporations, and the out-of-control globalization of the economy.

Emphasize Long-Term Aspects

It is difficult to structure and manage economic planning processes. Most people are indifferent to economics except when changes to the status quo threaten their own livelihoods or quality of life. These perceived threats can be particularly strong when people realize that the effects of a proposed development project will occur in their own back yards. One remedy for this problem is to involve the community in ways that emphasize the importance of long-term community or collective values rather than short-term individual interests. One way of defining a community is as a team of people working together in complementary and supportive roles. Community often includes open support of cultural diversity. Everybody is important when individuals work together.

Recognize and Accept the Need for Innovation and Change

Perhaps this is where we need the most profound adjustments. As we enter the new millennium, it becomes important to recognize and accept the need for changes in economies and the challenge of developing and promoting collective community decision-making processes. Some of these changes are exogenous, which means that the changes are caused by external influences outside the control of communities. But local involvement in economic decision making can also influence important choices. A process for planning economic development or a transition strategy can provide an opportunity to identify these choices.

Changes to the structure of the economy are occurring rapidly, and these changes are often difficult to understand and accept. We desperately need an ongoing and truthful examination of the economic changes and opportunities that are taking place in our communities, regions, provinces/states, and the world. Unfortunately, this has not been occurring. Instead, government usually produces heavily biased propaganda about how we need to protect existing jobs and the status quo, particularly in the traditional resource extraction industries. This information usually downplays the importance of other sectors of the economy, particularly tourism (the largest employer in the province), the rapidly growing high-technology industry, and the promising film-making industry.

Communicate

We also need to communicate information about the changes that are occurring in the economy to the public and especially to government decision makers. Graphic illustrations of comparative trends for different economic sectors could be as helpful to governments as they have been in the board rooms of industry. Credibility of information is essential. There is an excellent opportunity for academia to develop up-to-date information on all aspects of the changing economy and to disseminate this information to the public on a regular basis.

Mandate Ecosystem-Based Planning for all Levels of Government

Governments could develop more effective policies for land and resource-use planning, environmental management, and economic development before issuing permits for specific development projects. The *Municipal Act* could make economic and environmental planning mandatory for all municipal, regional district, and provincial planning processes. Communities may need help in dealing with the challenges of adapting to ecologically sustainable and ecosystem-based environmental management and to the complex changes to our economy. These new planning processes will need to incorporate true and effective public participation in decision-making processes. Public participation has to be much more than what usually happens, which is limited to providing government agencies with input that they either manipulate or ignore.

Eliminate Perverse Subsidies and Balance Government Spending Priorities

There is an immediate need to make major changes in government spending priorities. These changes include eliminating most, if not all, perverse subsidies to all economic sectors, but especially to the BC forest industry. (Figure 6 lists direct and indirect public costs of the BC forest industry.) Government's role is best limited to providing the necessary services and infrastructure to support economic development – services like education and health care, and infrastructure improvements such as rapid transit and bicycle and hiking trails.

Reduce the Allowable Annual Cut

Government is also responsible for insuring that the rate and methods of logging are ecologically sustainable. An immediate major reduction of the Allowable Annual Cut (AAC) is defensible from a conservation perspective, given the BC Ministry of Forests figures indicating that the AAC exceeds their estimate of the Long Run Sustained Yield by 28 percent (22 percent plus six percent to implement the Forest Practices Code), the detailed and well-founded recommendations of the Clayoquot Sound scientific advisory panel calling for a 62 percent reduction, and the Silva Foundation's extremely well-documented recommendation for a long-term reduction of 73 percent in the Slocan Valley. There have been other estimates in this ballpark, such as 1991 Forest Resource Commissioner Sandy Peels's call near the end of his investigation for a 50 percent reduction.

There is no doubt that we urgently need an immediate across-the-province reduction of 50 percent in the AAC. Later on, the government can calculate and implement additional reductions and/or adjustments for each particular area of the province.

The case for this action is strong, and the need is critical. First, detailed ecosystem-based planning in at least two areas of the province supports a reduction of 62 to 73 percent. Second, the experience in the Pacific northwest (Washington and Oregon) following the 47 percent reduction in logging in 1991 to protect the spotted owl was that the reduction actually benefited the overall economy. The number of jobs increased and average wages also went up. Around the world, governments have taken back tenures when they were not in the public interest. Third, according to several experts on this subject, including resource economist Richard Schwindt, lawyer Greg McDade, lawyer Mark Haddock, and political economist and lawyer Michael M'Gonigle, an across-the-province reduction for conservation would not require compensation under the existing law.

There is also a pressing need for a better balance of government expenditures among various services. While the forest, fishing, and mining industries have received many benefits from governments, growing and more promising segments of the BC economy have been disadvantaged in terms of government support staff, agency expenditures, and the burdens of taxation and regulation.

Support Sustainable Tourism

In the recent move from a line ministry to a Crown Corporation, Tourism BC's budget was reduced from $24 million to $17 million, while perverse subsidies for the ailing and ecologically unsustainable level of logging continued. As well as reducing funding for tourism services, the government also eliminated some tourism services altogether. Tourism is now the number one industry in the world ($4 trillion a year). The natural resources of BC offer a world-class resource for ecologically sound, nature-based tourism. Tourism is the largest employer of British Columbians. Twelve percent of the BC workforce is employed in tourism, over twice the percentage of workers in the forest industry.

Tourism is also the fastest growing industry on the planet. In 1996, tourism injected $7 billion into BC's economy, up 75 percent from $4 billion in 1990. Unlike the extractive industries, most tourism does not draw down our natural capital. Properly managed, tourism can be a sustainable land-based use of natural resources. Over the past decade, tourism-related job growth has increased by about 3.5 percent per year, three and a half times the rate of growth for the forest industry (Careless 1998).

Tourism BC has been weak in representing and protecting the interests of the tourism industry. This is partly due to the low priority government gives to tourism. While government spending on forestry is about 10 percent of the provincial gross domestic product (GDP) generated by the forest industry, government spending on tourism is only 0.5 percent of the GDP generated by the tourism industry. In terms of government employment, the Ministry of Forests employs 4,470 people compared to only 72 people employed by Tourism BC and 370 by BC Parks.

Tourism is not the only fast growing industry in the province. The high-tech and film industries, although smaller in size in relation to the tourism industry, are growing at an even faster rate. In a way, these up and coming industries are even more important to the province than tourism. This is because tourism is a tertiary industry; it depends on other sectors of the economy to generate income.

Support Appropriate High-Tech Industry

Between 1990 and 1997, the annual production of the high-tech sector increased by an average of nearly 7%, roughly three times the annual growth rate of the entire economy. The number of people employed by high-tech companies has nearly doubled since 1990 (Economic Analysis of B.C., August, 1999). In 1998, exports of electrical/electronic products rose 11 percent. Industry leaders predict BC has the potential to add 10,000 high-tech jobs every year; they predict that this sector could employ more workers than the forest industry within just five years. High-tech employment pays well. The average high-tech worker in Washington State earned $81,000 US (about $120,000 Canadian) during 1998. High-tech jobs are "footloose." Workers in this industry change jobs often and are often attracted by the high quality of living of BC's communities (Careless, 1998). Ballard Power (Chapter 13) is worth twice the value of MacMillan Bloedel on the Toronto Stock Exchange, is rapidly growing, and has fantastic economic and environmental potential. Yet Ballard Power has been given relatively little in government subsidies compared with MacMillan Bloedel and other large forest companies.

Conclusion

It makes neither ecological nor economic sense to continue the massive government subsidies to the forest industry. If BC taxpayers were aware of the magnitude of this subsidy, I predict that about 90 percent of them would want to eliminate it or at least substantially reduce it. Only those working in the forest industry (5.5 percent of the work force) would want to continue the subsidies that benefit them.

It makes good sense to manage BC's natural resources in a way that benefits the growing tourism industry and maintains the relatively high quality of life that benefits all British Columbians. Managing natural resources this way will especially benefit those drawn to the province to work in the growing high-tech and film industries and those who want to retire here (and spend their substantial retirement income and savings). An example of this type of resource management is the proposed expansion and budget increase for BC Parks, an investment that Coopers and Lybrand say will show a return of $9 for every dollar spent.

Government should not be afraid to make adjustments. The Pacific northwest states of Washington and Oregon recently made changes similar to those needed in BC. The Pacific northwest economy has benefited from these changes with increased employment, higher wages, and better environmental management.

I believe in community planning. I have been actively involved both as a professional planner and volunteer advocate planner for most of my adult life. From my experience, I believe that the people who live closest to economic development projects will make the best long-term recommendations and decisions, and, if allowed to do so, local communities will usually make better policy for environmental management and economic development. There are exceptions to this preference for local control – such as development and environmental protection that has more than local significance. The provincial and national park systems are one example of land use that transcends community and even provincial preferences. Preserving biological and cultural diversity and protecting endangered species are other examples of values that have more than local significance. Legislation that specifies different requirements for complementary levels of planning and public decision making can incorporate the need to address these and other issues.

If we hope to make a difference, we need to make these changes now. We don't have any time to lose.

References

Armstrong, Jeannette 1996. *"Sharing One Skin"*: Okanagan Community, *The Case Against the Global Economy and for a Turn Toward the Local*. Sierra Club Books.

Ballard Power Systems 1999. 1998 Annual Report.

Ballard Power Systems 1998. 1997 Annual Report.

Boyd, David 1998. The Nisga'a Treaty: Towards a Sustainable Future? Newsletter published by the Northwest Institute for Bioregional Research.

BC Jobs Protection Commissioner 1998. Fishing for Money.

BC Parks 1976. Interim Policy Statement for Mt. Edizza.

BC Parks 1980. Spatsizi Plateau Wilderness Park Master Plan.

BC Parks 1976. Interim Policy Statement for Mr. Edizza.

BC Parks 1991. Stikine River Recreation Area Interim Management Statement.

BC Parks 1997. Stikine Country Protected Areas Interim Recreation Management Statement.

BC Wild 1998. Overcut, British Columbia's Forest Policy and the Liquidation of Old-Growth Forests, Parts I, II and III.

Beuter, J.H. 1995. Legacy and Promise: Oregon's Forests and Wood Products Industry. Oregon Business Council and Oregon Forest Resources Institute.

Beuter, J.H. 1998. Legacy and Promise: Oregon's Forests and Wood Products Industry (Revised and Updated). Oregon Business Council and the Oregon Forest Resources Institute.

British Columbia Government 1998. Protected Areas Strategy Update.

British Columbia Government 1999. Status Report: British Columbia's Economic Plan.

British Columbia Government 1999. Economic Update.

Broadhead, John 1995. Gwaii Haanas Transitions Study. Haida Gwaii Museum.

Brown, Ron 1995. Would you Want Your Kid to Work Here? A report on retraining and educational needs of British Columbia Sawmill Workers prepared for IWA Canada, Local 1-3567 and Douglas College.

Burda, Cheri, Deborah Curran, Fred Gale, and Michael M'Gonigle 1997. Forests in Trust: Reforming British Columbia's Forest Tenure System for Ecosystem and Community Health, a report produced by the Eco-Research Chair of Environmental Law and Policy, Faculty of Law and School of Environmental Studies, University of Victoria.

Canadian Press and Associated Press, 1999. Auto Giant Makes Major Gains Using Ballard Fuel Cell, Vancouver Sun

Capra, Fritjof 1996. *The Web of Life, A New Scientific Understanding of Living Systems*. Anchor Books

Careless, Ric 1997. *To Save the Wild Earth, Field Notes from the Environmental Frontline*. Raincoast Books.

Careless, Ric 1998, Jobs and Environment Action Plan.

Cassiar Iskut-Stikine LRMP 1998. Draft Zone Summaries for Scenario Anaysis.

City of Redmond, 1970. Optimum Land Use Plan.

Clark, M. 1994. Oregon Employment and Payrolls. Oregon Employment Department.

Clarke, Tony 1996. *Mechanisms of Corporate Rule, The Case Against the Global Economy and for a Turn Toward the Local*. Sierra Club Books.

Cohen, Couture Associates and Don R. Allen and Associates 1988, Forest Sector Labour Force Adjustment Study, prepared for Employment and Immigration Canada, Industry, Science and Technology Canada, Labour Canada, and Ministry of State (Forestry).

Collaborative Committee for the 1991-1994 Conservation Potential Review 1994. Electricity Conservation Potential Review 1988-2010: Phase II – Achievable Conservation Potential Through Technological and Operating Change.

Commission on Resources and Environment 1994, Vancouver Island Land Use Plan and West Kootenay-Boundary Land Use Plan.

Connelly, Dolly 1970. "Great Escape Living on Portage Bay." *American Home*.

Coopers and Lybrand Consulting 1996. Current and Future Economic Benefits of British Columbia Parks. Report for the British Columbia Ministry of Environment, Lands and Parks.

Copeland, Grant 1969. "A Common Pride Among the Residents." *Seattle Times*.

Copeland, Grant 1969. Improving Neighborhood Identity and Personal Involvement in Residential Areas - An Experiment in Environmental Design, Implementation and Ex-Post-Facto Evaluation, unpublished MA thesis, University of Washington.

Copeland, Grant 1969. Interim Housing Study, an Analysis of the Housing Market in the Redmond Planning Area, an unpublished planning department staff report prepared for the City of Redmond.

Copeland, Grant 1970. Ecological Analysis of the Redmond Planning Area, an unpublished planning department staff report prepared for the City of Redmond.

Copeland, Grant 1970. Redmond Watershed Study, an unpublished study prepared for the City of Redmond.

Copeland, Grant 1993. Anhluut'ukwsim Laxmihl Angwinga'asanskwhl Nisga'a / Nisga'a Memorial Lava Bed Park Draft Master Plan, prepared for the Joint Nisga'a / BC Parks Management Committee and subsequently published by BC Parks 1998.

Copeland, Grant 1994. Nelson in Transition, An Economic Case Study, an unpublished report prepared for BC Wild, The Conservation Alliance of British Columbia.

Copeland, Grant 1994. Nisga'a Tourism Study, a confidential report prepared for the Nisga'a Tribal Council.

Copeland, Grant 1994. Retallack Alpine Adventures, Ltd. Conceptual Development Plan, Feasibility Assessment, and Financing Plan, unpublished confidential study.

Copeland, Grant 1995. An Economic Transition Strategy for the Slocan Valley, an unpublished report prepared for BC Wild, The Conservation Alliance of British Columbia.

Copeland, Grant 1996. Nisga'a Conceptual Backcountry Tourism Development Plan, a confidential report prepared for the Nisga'a Tribal Council.

Copeland, Grant 1996. Retallack Alpine Adventures, Ltd. Management Plan, unpublished report submitted to BC Lands.

Copeland, Grant 1997. Huchsduwachsdu Nuyem Jees / Kitlope Heritage Conservancy Draft Background Document, unpublished report prepared for the Kitlope Management Committee.

Copeland, Grant 1998. Nisga'a Commercial Recreation Project Management Plan, unpublished report prepared for the Nisga'a Tribal Council submitted to BC Lands.

Copeland, Grant and Steve Nicol 1998. Economic Opportunities and Barriers Study Final Report for the Cassiar Iskut-Stikine LRMP. Report distributed to LRMP table members.

Copeland, Grant, Wayne McCrory, and Ray Travers 1992. The Greater Kitlope Ecosystem: A Wilderness Planning Framework, Haisla Nation and Ecotrust.

Costanza, Robert, editor 1991. *Ecological Economics, the Science and Management of Sustainability*. Columbia University Press.

Daly, Herman E. and John B. Cobb Jr. 1989. *For the Common Good, Redirecting the Economy Toward Community, the Environment, and a Sustainable Future*. Beacon Press.

Davis, Wade 1998. *The Clouded Leopard, Travels to Landscapes of Spirit and Desire*. Douglas and McIntyre.

De Moor, A.P.G. 1997. Subsidizing Unsustainable Development: Undermining the Earth with Public Funds. The Earth Council, San Jose, Costa Rica.

Divorak, Elinor and Linda Barker 1994. Harmony Foundation, personal communication.

Durning, Alan Thein and Yoram Bauman 1998. *Tax Shift*. Northwest Environment Watch.

Economist February 29, 1993. "The Final Frontier."

Economic Analysis of BC August, 1999. Newsletter of the Savings and Credit Unions of BC.

Environment Canada 1985. Heritage for Tomorrow, Proceedings of the Canadian Assembly on National Parks and Protected Areas, A National Parks Centennial Project.

Forest Resources Commission 1991. The Future of Our Forests. Government of British Columbia.

Friends of the Stikine 1985. A Visitor Guide to the Stikine, Second Edition with Topographic Map and National Park Reserve Proposal.

Galbraith, John Kenneth 1967. *The New Industrial State*. Houghton Mifflin Company.

Gale, Robert, Fred Gale, and Tom Green 1999. Accounting for the Forests, a Methodological Critique of Price Waterhouses's Report "The Forest Industry in British Columbia 1997," published by the Sierra Club of BC.

Glavin, Terry and Dan Edwards. *Set Adrift*. David Suzuki Foundation. May 1999.

Globe and Mail, July 12, 1999. "Canada Again Tops Survey as Best Place to Live"

Goetz, Emily, B. Bent, and S. Sharpe 1991. A Preliminary Study of Job-Related Communications Skills in British Columbia Sawmills, report prepared for Council of Forest Industries and IWA-Canada.

Goldsmith, Edward 1996. *The Last Word: Family, Community, Democracy, The Case Against the Global Economy and for a Turn Toward the Local*. Sierra Club Books.

Goldsmith, Edward and Nicholas Hildyard 1984. *The Social and Environmental Effects of Large Dams*. Sierra Club Books.

Gosnell, Joseph 1998. Speech delivered to the 36th Parliament, Official Report of the Debates of the British Columbia Legislative Assembly.

Greater Vancouver Regional District and the Province of BC 1993. Transport 2021, A Long-Range Transportation Plan for Greater Vancouver.

Hammond, Herb 1991. Seeing the Forest Among the Trees, the Case for Wholistic Forest Use. Polestar.

Haynes, R.W. and A. L. Horne. 1997. Chapter 6: "Economic Assessment of the Basin." *Assessment of Ecosystem Components in the Interior Columbia Basin and Portions of the Klamath and Great Basins*, Volume IV. Edited by T.M. Quigley and S.J. Arbelbide. General Technical Report PNW-GTR-405, OR: U.S. Department of Agriculture, Forest Service, Pacific Northwest Research Station. June. Pages 1715-1869.

Haynes, R.W., N.A. Bolon, and D.T. Hormachea 1992. The Economic Impact on the Forest Sector of Critical Habitat Delineation for Salmon in the Columbia and Snake River Basin. U.S. Department of Agriculture, Forest Service, Pacific Northwest Research Station. General Technical Report. PNW-GTR-307.

Henley, Thom 1989. *Rediscovery, Ancient Pathways – New Directions, A Guidebook to Outdoor Education*. Western Canada Wilderness Committee.

Hummel, Monte, 1989. *Endangered Spaces, The Future for Canada's Wilderness*, Key Porter Books, Ltd.

Hunter, Justine 1999. "Home Depot Gives Green Light to Forest Products Certification." *Vancouver Sun*.

Hydroxyl Systems 1999. Company Profile and Product Descriptions.

Kootenay Resource Management Committee and Regional District of Central Kootenay 1983. Slocan Valley Plan, A Land Use and Economic Plan for the Slocan Valley Part I: Policies and Implementation Measures.

Korten, David C 1996. *The Failures of Bretton Woods, The Case Against the Global Economy and for a Turn Toward the Local*. Sierra Club Books.

Lacroix, Bruce 1994. Personal communication.

Legacy Panel 1998. Interim Report of the Legacy Panel, BC's Park Legacy Project.

Lerner, Michael 1986. *Surplus Powerlessness, the Psychodynamics of Everyday Life and the Psychology of Individual and Social Transformation*. Humanities Press International, Inc.

M'Gonigle, Michael 1999. "Ecological Economics and Political Ecology: Towards a Necessary Synthesis." Soon to be published in *Ecological Economics*.

M'Gonigle, Michael and Ben Parfitt 1994. *Forestopia, A Practical Guide to the New Forest Economy*. Harbor Publishing.

MacIsaac, Ron and Anne Champagne 1994. *Clayoquot Mass Trials*. New Society Publishers.

Major, Michael 1999. Personal communication.

Mander, Jerry 1996. *The Rules of Corporate Behavior, The Case Against the Global Economy and for a Turn Toward the Local*. Sierra Club Books.

Mander, Jerry and Edward Goldsmith, editors 1996. *The Case Against the Global Economy and for a Turn Toward the Local*. Sierra Club Books.

McHarg, Ian L. 1969. *Design with Nature*. Natural History Press.

Marchak, M. Patricia, Scott L. Aycock and Deborah M. Herbert 1999. *Falldown: Forest Policy in British Columbia*. The David Suzuki Foundation and Ecotrust Canada.

Mascall, Michael and Barbara Campbell 1997. Public Investment by Governments in the BC Forest Industry 1988/89 to 1995/96. Unpublished report prepared for BC Wild.

May, Elizabeth 1998. *At the Cutting Edge, The Crisis in Canada's Forests*. Key Porter Books.

May, Elizabeth 1998. "National Office Report," The Sierra Report. Sierra Club in Western Canada.

Ministry of Forests 1989. Lower Stikine Management Plan.

Moore, Keith 1991. Coastal Watersheds, An Inventory of Watersheds in the Coastal Temperate Forests of British Columbia. Earthlife Canada Foundation and Ecotrust/Conservation International.

Morton, Peter 1999. "Home Depot to Phase Out 'Endangered' Lumber, *Financial Post*. August 27, 1999.

Myers, Norman June 1998. "Has the World Gone Mad?" *Guardian*.

Myers, N. and J. Kent 1998. Perverse Subsidies: Taxes Undercutting Our Economies and Environments Alike. International Institute for Sustainable Development, Manitoba, Canada.

Nader, Ralph and William Taylor 1986. *The Big Boys, Power and Position in American Business*. Pantheon Books.

National Geographic January 1998 "Making Sense of the Millennium." May 1998 "Unlocking the Climate Puzzle." October 1998 "Population." and February 1999 "Biodiversity, The Fragile Web."

Natural Resources Management Program, Simon Fraser University 1990. Wilderness and Forestry: Assessing the Cost of Comprehensive Wilderness Protection in British Columbia, SFU-NRM Report No. 6.

Niemi, Ernie, and Andrew Johnston 1999. The Sky Did Not Fall: The Pacific Northwest's Response to Logging Reductions. Sierra Club of British Columbia.

Nikkei Business Magazine 1998. Special Feature: "The Future of the Automobile."

Nisga'a Nation, Canada, British Columbia 1998. *Nisga'a Final Agreement*.

Norberg-Hodge 1996. *Shifting Direction: From Global Dependence to Local Interdependence, The Case Against the Global Economy and for a Turn Toward the Local*. Sierra Club Books.

Ochs, John 1999. Personal communication.

Olson, D. 1990. Economic Impacts of the ISC Northern Spotted Owl Conservation Strategy for Washington, Oregon, and Northern California. University of Minnesota.

Pacific Northwest Economists 1995. Economic Well-Being and Environmental Protection in the Pacific Northwest.

Pearse, Tony 1998. Nisga'a Treaty Highlights, newsletter published by the Northwest Institute for Bioregional Research.

Pinkerton, Evelyn 1989. *Co-Operative Management of Local Fisheries: New Directions for Improved Management and Community Development*. University of British Columbia Press.

Power, Thomas Michael 1988. *The Economic Pursuit of Quality*. M. E. Sharpe, Inc.

Power, Thomas Michael 1996. *Lost Landscapes and Failed Economies, The Search for a Value of Place*. Island Press.

Puget Sound Regional Council 1995. 1995 Metropolitan Transportation Plan.

Purvis, Andrew 1999. "Whose Home and Native Land?" Time Magazine.

Rasker, Raymond 1993. "Rural Development, Conservation, and Public Policy in the Greater Yellowstone Ecosystem." *Society and Natural Resources*, UK.

Rasker, Raymond 1994. "A New Look at Old Vistas: The Economic Role of Environmental Quality in Western Public Lands." University of Colorado *Law Review*.

Rasker, Ray, Julie Fox Gorte, and Carolyn Alkire 1997. Logging National Forests to Create Jobs: An Unworkable Covenant. A paper published by the Wilderness Society.

Reich, Robert B. 1991. *The Work of Nations*, Vintage Books.

Rudzitis, Gundars and Harley E. Johansen Spring 1989. "Migration into Western Wilderness Counties: Causes and Consequences." W. Wildlands.

Schallau, C., W. Maki, and J. Beuter 1969. "Economic Impact Projections for Alternative Levels of Timber Production in the Douglas-Fir Region." *Annals of Regional Science* 3 (1).

Sierra July-August 1999. "Logging our Legacy: Our National Forests Belong to Us. So Why Are they on the Auction Block?" The Magazine of the Sierra Club.

Sierra Legal Defense Fund May 1999. Newsletter No. 22.

Silva Forest Foundation 1996. An Ecosystem-Based Landscape Plan for the Slocan River Watershed, report and maps.

Slocan Valley Community Forest Management Project 1974. Final Report

Slocan Valley Planning Program 1981. Technical Reports on Water Resources and Watersheds, Vacant Crown Land Outside Provincial Forests, Air and Water Quality, Wildlife,Recreational Analysis, Population and Labour Force Analysis, Heritage Resources, Tourism Analysis, Agricultural Resource Study, Economic Opportunities Study, Rural Community Profiles, and Results of Series 1 Public Meetings June 1-4, 1981.

Slocan Valley Planning Program 1982. Technical Report on Tourism Analysis Phase II.

Snepenger, David J., Jerry D. Johnson, and Raymond Rasker 1995. "Travel-Stimulated entrepreneurial Migration."

Swerdlow, Joel L. February 1999. "Biodiversity, The Fragile Web." *National Geographic*.

Time Magazine November 1997. "Our Precious Planet, Why Saving the Environment Will be the Next Century's Biggest Challenge."

Thurlow, Lester C. 1993. Head to Head.

Travers, O.R., R. Marsh, T. Vold, J. van Barneveld, S. Haawthorn, and W. Yeomans 1981. Resources of the Slocan Valley

Travers, Ray 1991. A Cultural and Scientific Reconnaissance of the Greater Kitlope Ecosystem. Haisla Nation and Ecotrust.

US Department of Agriculture 1988. Final Supplement to the Environmental Impact Statement for an Amendment to the Pacific Northwest Regional Guide, Volume 1, Spotted Owl Guidelines. Pacific Northwest Regional Office.

Utzig, Greg and Mark Walmsley 1988. Evaluation of Soil Degradation as a Factor Affecting Forest Productivity in BC: A Problem Analysis. FRDA Report 25.

Valhalla Society 1991. BC's Endangered Wilderness, A Comprehensive Proposal for Protection.

Valhalla Society, 1995. Major Changes for Retallack/Jackson Basin, Educational Bulletin No.25.

Vancouver *Province* May 27, 1999. "$110 m to Skeena" and "Report Rips Salmon Policy."

Vancouver *Province* August 19, 1999. "Habitat Tab $4B."

Vancouver *Sun* 1999. "Paper, Forestry Shares Lead TSE."

Washington State Land Planning Commission 1974, Proposed Substitute House Bill 791, submitted to the Washington State Legislature.

Whitewater Ski Resort Ltd. 1994. Whitewater Market Facts.

Wolf, R.E, 1994. Receipt Outlay Analysis of U.S. Forest Service Timber Sales Program. 1983-1994.

World Commission on Environment and Development 1987. *Our Common Future*. Oxford University Press.

Grant Copeland is a planning consultant and entrepreneur. He received a BA in Business Administration from Washington State University and a Master of Urban Planning from the University of Washington. He has 30 years experience working for most levels of government in the US and Canada and many First Nations in British Columbia and the Yukon. His innovative economic development projects in the US and Canada have been widely published. Before he immigrated to Canada in 1973, he was assistant director of the Washington State Land Planning Commission. Grant has spent a substantial part of his life doing volunteer work for environmental organizations. He was a founding director of the Valhalla Society in BC and currently serves on the boards of the Sierra Club of BC and the Friends of the Stikine. He was born in Yakima, Washington, and lives in New Denver, British Columbia.

New Society Publishers' mission is to publish books that contribute in fundamental ways to building an ecologically sustainable and just society, and to do so with the least possible impact on the environment in a manner that models that vision.

If you have enjoyed *Acts of Balance: Profits, People and Place*, you may also want to check out our other titles in the following categories:

Progressive Leadership
Ecological Design & Planning
Environment & Justice
New Forestry
Accountable Economics
Conscientious Commerce
Resistance & Community
Educational & Parenting Resources

For a full list of NSP's titles, please call 1·800·567·6772
or check out our web site at:
www.newsociety.com

NEW SOCIETY PUBLISHERS